the unoffendable heart

Books by Mike Signorelli

Inherit Your Freedom

Fire Starters

The Unoffendable Heart

the unoffendable heart

breaking free from the cycle of offense to live in freedom, love, and forgiveness

Mike Signorelli

Chosen
a division of Baker Publishing Group
Minneapolis, Minnesota

Published by Chosen Books
Minneapolis, Minnesota
ChosenBooks.com

Chosen Books is a division of
Baker Publishing Group, Grand Rapids, Michigan

Library of Congress Cataloging-in-Publication Data
Names: Signorelli, Mike author
Title: The unoffendable heart : breaking free from the cycle of offense to live in freedom, love, and forgiveness / Mike Signorelli.
Description: Minneapolis, Minnesota : Chosen, a division of Baker Publishing Group, [2026] | Includes bibliographical references.
Identifiers: LCCN 2026006878 | ISBN 9780800772611 paperback | ISBN 9781493456635 ebook
Subjects: LCSH: Healing—Religious aspects—Christianity | Love—Religious aspects—Christianity | Forgiveness—Religious aspects—Christianity
Classification: LCC BT732 .S497 2026
LC record available at https://lccn.loc.gov/2026006878

Cover design by David Carlson, Studio Gearbox

Baker Publishing Group publications use paper produced from sustainable forestry practices and postconsumer waste whenever possible.

26 27 28 29 30 31 32 7 6 5 4 3 2 1

To my beautiful wife, Julie Lauren Signorelli,
whose seventy-times-seven mercy led me into
the freedom of an unoffendable heart

contents

Foreword by John Bevere 9

Introduction: Offense Edits Your Entire Life 11

Part One: The Wounded Heart 21

1. The Heart of the Matter: A Call to Adventure 23
2. Expectations: The Ledger of Disappointment 35
3. Justice: Why Your Heart Keeps Score 45
4. Confidence: The Fear of People's Opinions 63
5. Memory: The Past That Won't Let Go 85

Part Two: The Healing Process 99

6. Going Deep into the Heart 101
7. Resurrection of the Heart 127
8. Surrender Is Not a Sidenote 139

Part Three: The Healed Heart 151

9. Scars Are Signs of Life 153
10. Joining the Mission 161

Epilogue: The Healed Heart, the Unexpected Story 179

Notes 183

foreword

Jesus gave a sobering warning about the days leading up to His return. When His disciples asked about the signs of the end, He first explained what would take place externally—wars, rumors of wars, natural disasters, trials, and deception through false christs. Then He described what would take place internally—the condition of the human heart: "Many will be offended, will betray one another, and will hate one another. . . . And because lawlessness will abound, the love of many will grow cold" (Matthew 24:10–12 NKJV). Notice the internal progression—offense leads to betrayal, betrayal leads to hatred, and hatred ultimately produces cold hearts.

Offense is one of the enemy's most subtle and effective weapons to entrap believers. It often begins with a legitimate hurt—yet if left unresolved, it quietly poisons our hearts, divides relationships, and dulls our love for God and others.

The truth is, the opportunity to be offended will come. It's not a matter of *if* we encounter it, but *when*. So the real question is, *What will we do with it?* In these last days, opportunities to be offended are everywhere. If we are not diligently watching and praying, the bait is easy to take.

This is why Mike Signorelli's message in *The Unoffendable Heart* is so timely and important. Mike doesn't ignore the reality of pain or betrayal; he confronts it head on while pointing us to the higher way of Christ. With clarity and pastoral insight, he reminds us that forgiveness is not weakness—it is freedom. To live unoffendable is not to pretend wounds don't exist, but to refuse to allow those wounds to harden our hearts.

An unoffendable heart is a guarded heart—not to be mistaken for a hardened one. It's a heart that chooses love over bitterness and freedom over bondage. Living unoffendable keeps our hearts tender before God and protects the very thing Jesus warned could grow cold—our love. In a world filled with outrage, division, and offense, believers who walk in forgiveness will stand out like lights in the darkness.

I believe this book speaks directly to the deep needs of our time. The pressures of the days we're living in call for believers to resist becoming offended. As you read these pages, my prayer is that the Holy Spirit will gently search your heart, bring healing where it's needed, and lead you into the freedom that comes through forgiveness.

The days ahead will require strong hearts—and one of the strongest hearts you can have is an unoffendable one.

John Bevere, bestselling author and minister,
co-founder of Messenger International and MessengerX

introduction

offense edits your entire life

The city was loud that day, louder than usual, or maybe my nerves just made it feel that way.

Car horns tangled into a kind of urban symphony—the modern kind that sounds chaotic—punctuated by the hiss of bus brakes and the hum of a thousand conversations colliding on the sidewalks. Food carts let off waves of steam that smelled like pretzels, roasted nuts, and street meat, mixed in with odors from sewers and the sweat of New York City. Somewhere down the block, a saxophone played just sharp enough to sound off-key.

I was in Manhattan, and the whole world looked as if it was moving forward. But I wasn't. I was flooded, about to have a Manhattan meltdown.

It didn't take much—a single careless word, a moment that would seem trivial to anyone else—and suddenly, I wasn't standing on a street. I was standing in fire.

My chest tightened as though invisible straps had been cinched across me. Breathing felt shallow, rushed, as though I couldn't pull enough oxygen into my lungs. My fists were clenched so tightly that my fingernails pressed little half-moon marks into my palms. My jaw locked until I could feel the grind of my teeth. And my thoughts? They weren't logical. They weren't careful. They were barbed wires snapping across my mind: *How dare they? I can't believe this. I'm done.*

Here's what makes it worse: I can't even tell you what set me off. I know it wasn't monumental. It wasn't a betrayal worthy of the explosion it caused in my chest. It was a spark, barely visible, yet it landed on years of dry timber I hadn't dealt with.

From the outside, I probably looked like any other New Yorker standing on the sidewalk. But on the inside, I was unraveling. I was consumed.

That's what offense does.

It doesn't ask your permission. It doesn't wait until you're ready. It finds the pile of unspoken expectations, unhealed disappointments, and buried frustrations.

And then, with one spark, the whole thing ignites.

I wish I could say I caught myself, that I paused long enough to breathe, that I prayed or remembered Scripture in that moment.

But I didn't. I let it run. I let the fire spread. I carried that blaze with me the rest of the day. Every conversation I had was tinted by it. Every look from a stranger was interpreted through it.

Offense had taken the driver's seat, and I was just along for the ride.

And here's the part that stung the most when I looked back later: It felt powerful at first. There's a rush when you give yourself over to offense, a false sense of strength. Your heart pounds, adrenaline surges, and you think, *This will protect me. This will keep me from being hurt again.*

But it's a lie. That fire doesn't protect. It consumes. It doesn't guard your heart. It burns it.

And maybe you've been there. Maybe not in Manhattan, but in your kitchen, your office, your church lobby. A small spark lit up the dry brush of your soul, and before you could catch it, the whole thing was ablaze.

Scripture has a way of naming what we can't. When Cain grew furious that God had accepted Abel's offering and not his, the Lord warned him: "Sin is crouching at your door; it desires to have you, but you must rule over it" (Genesis 4:7 NIV). That's the nature of offense. It crouches at the door. It waits for a chance to pounce. And if you don't have a plan, if you don't have a way to master it—it will master you.

That day in Manhattan, offense mastered me. And the truth is, I didn't even realize it until later.

If you've lived more than a minute, you know what I'm talking about. Offense doesn't need a public stage. It doesn't wait for a courtroom drama or a televised debate. It happens in kitchens, in text threads, in boardrooms, and yes, even in the church lobby.

It might look like this: You send a text, something you thought was simple, even kind, and hours pass. No reply. Then you notice the person posted a story on Instagram. So there's time for that, but not for you?

That burn in your chest?

That's offense.

Or maybe you show up to a family dinner and realize decisions were made without you. Your brother is already praying over the meal. Your sister has already portioned out who's bringing what for Thanksgiving. Nobody asked for your input. Nobody noticed you. It feels small, but the sting is real.

Or it's at work. You've been pulling long hours, carrying the extra load, keeping the project afloat. Then the boss congratulates someone else in the meeting. Someone who barely did a fraction of what you did.

Your jaw sets. You smile, but the smile is paper-thin.

And then there's church. (Surely we wouldn't take offense in the Lord's house!) You're faithful, serving, giving, showing up early to stack chairs or sing or watch the toddlers in the nursery. Then someone else, someone newer, less invested, gets the recognition. That person is asked to pray. He or she is invited onto the leadership team.

You shake hands on Sunday, but inside? You're offended.

None of these scenarios are front-page news. They don't make headlines. But they make scars. They change how you walk into a room, how you read a text, how quickly you trust. Offense has a way of editing your entire life.

Everyday Offense

If you look closely, you see this issue everywhere. One word or disrespectful act can spark something much bigger. Have you heard how World War I began? It started with an offense. A series of offenses led to murder. The assassination of Archduke Franz Ferdinand in 1914 seemed like a political event, but it was tied to years of anger and distrust. One bullet ignited the fuse, leading to a world war.

Today, we live in a similar situation, but it's digital. A careless comment can trigger viral outrage. A 30-second video cuts someone's words out of context, and suddenly millions are offended for people they don't even know. Maybe you've found yourself scrolling late at night, feeling upset over something you can't change.

It's almost funny, isn't it? We have apps to help us "connect," yet they often just lead to more offense.

I'll admit, sometimes I think I'm above it all. Maybe you do too. You tell yourself, *I don't get caught in petty drama.* Then someone posts something passive-aggressive, and you know it's aimed at you.

Or you see friends hanging out without you, and it hurts in a way you didn't expect. Suddenly, you feel like that lonely kid, sitting alone at lunch, offended all over again.

It doesn't matter how "mature" you think you are. The fire doesn't care. If there are old wounds or buried insecurities inside you, the fire will find them. When it does, it won't just burn the surface; it will change you.

That's why these little moments matter. They add up like dry brush in a forest. Then one spark, one word, one mistake, and everything goes up in flames.

You know this because you've lived it. And if we're honest, some of us are experiencing it right now.

A Cultural Firestorm

I'm writing this during a cultural moment. Just last week, Charlie Kirk was assassinated onstage. He was speaking, doing what leaders do—sharing convictions, trying to persuade, stepping into the public square—and a man, overcome by something burning in him, raised a gun and pulled the trigger. Just like that, a single mom was made. Children will grow up without their father.

By the time you are reading this, we may know all the motives. We may never know every thought that ran through the shooter's mind. But it's safe to say this: He was offended by someone he didn't even know personally. Deeply offended. Enough that he believed cold-blooded murder was justified.

That's what offense does when it grows unchecked. It starts small, but in the end, it kills.

Then something else happened. Almost immediately, the fire spread beyond that stage.

Some people called it karma. A teacher typed that word out for the world to see, as though a bullet to the neck were the natural consequence of speaking your mind.

Others mocked Charlie Kirk at vigils, using the moment of mourning to make jokes.

Online, I watched the tone shift almost instantly from grief to sarcasm, as if the tragedy were just another meme to be recycled.

Politicians rushed in. One declared that we needed to "beat the hell out of radical left lunatics." Another representative blamed the media outright, calling all journalists complicit, as though their reporting had pulled the trigger. (Some of it was probably a contributing factor, but not all.)

And then the rumors started. Claims that the bullets had slogans on them. Claims that the shooter was part of one group or another, tied to conspiracies that spread faster than facts. None of it confirmed, but all of it repeated by the mobs.

The fire leapt from one heart to millions.

Here's the part that struck me: Compassion barely had time to breathe. But harsh words became wind on the open fire.

It took less than a day for outrage to drown out grief. Before the body was even buried, words were flying like shrapnel. Posts, counter-posts, sound bites, hashtags. It was as if the very oxygen of our culture had been saturated with offense, and all it took was this spark for the whole nation to ignite.

And if you step back, doesn't it feel orchestrated? Doesn't it seem as if someone, or something, feeds on this cycle?

The Bible says, "For we do not wrestle against flesh and blood, but against the rulers, against the authorities, against the cosmic powers over this present darkness" (Ephesians 6:12). I believe that.

What happened on that stage was more than politics. What happened online afterward was more than commentary. Offense was weaponized. The enemy used it to divide, to provoke, to blind. He used the offendable hearts of humanity in a fallen world and set a fire.

And the media? They fed it. (Again, not all, but enough.) They know offense keeps us watching, scrolling, refreshing. Sensational headlines, amplified outrage, hot takes designed to keep the fire going. It may sound harsh, but it appears that outrage has become an economy. And we are its currency.

Think about it.

One man's offense led to a murder.

Millions of people's offense turned mourning into mockery.

Institutions, schools, universities, and workplaces fired or suspended people because their words about Charlie Kirk were so charged, so offensive, that they themselves became stories.

And what are we left with? A man is dead, a family is grieving, and a nation is in a rage-filled cage fight.

This is the demonic nature of offense. It doesn't just hurt feelings. It doesn't just strain friendships. Left unchecked, it kills, it divides, it multiplies, until entire societies are engulfed.

You may not see yourself in the shooter. Maybe you'd never imagine crossing that line. But can you see yourself in the aftershocks? Posting something snarky. Celebrating when someone you disagree with falls. Sharing an article you didn't fact-check because it confirmed what you already felt. Ending friendships forever?

If we're honest, most of us can.

And that's why I can't gloss over this moment. Because what happened with Charlie Kirk is not just news. It's a mirror. It's showing us what offense does when it gets everything it wants.

We'll go deeper into this later. We'll talk about the spiritual dimension—how offense is a portal the enemy uses to sow division in churches, marriages, friendships, even nations. We'll talk about how Satan doesn't need new weapons when this one works so well.

But for now, I want you to see it clearly: Offense is not harmless. It is not trivial. It is not just "being sensitive." It is fire. And when it runs its course, it consumes everything in its path.

Stop, Drop, and Roll

When I was a kid, the school would run fire drills. You probably experienced the same ones. The alarm would shriek, and we'd shuffle out into the hallway, single file, hands at our sides. Dick Van Dyke and our teachers drilled it into us: *Stop. Drop. And Roll, Baby, Roll.*

If your clothes ever caught fire, you didn't run screaming through the building; you stopped moving, dropped to the ground, and rolled until the flames went out. Simple. Memorable.

The logic was clear. In a crisis, you won't have time to think. You need muscle memory. You need something so basic that it overrides panic.

We had a drill for our bodies, but no one ever gave us a drill for our hearts. So when offense comes, and it always comes, we panic.

We don't stop; we sprint straight into the flames. We don't drop what we're carrying; we pile on expectations, anger, blame. We don't roll forward into freedom; we collapse backward into seething resentment and rage.

And here's the sad part: Some of us have been living that way for years. Every relationship singed. Every disagreement turning into a slow burn. Every disappointment smoldering beneath the surface until the next spark hits.

Wouldn't it be something if we had a way to stop the fire before it consumed us? If we had a drill simple enough to remember in panic, strong enough to save a heart from added pain?

That's what this book is for. It's not a slogan or a pep talk. It's your fire drill for the soul. It's how you survive the mental, emotional, and spiritual dangers of the day.

The Unoffendable Life

Now imagine your life without the fire.

You wake up tomorrow and the spark still comes. Your spouse snaps, your boss overlooks you, your friend forgets. But instead of your chest tightening and your mind racing, something else happens. You notice the offense, but you don't take it in. You let it fall. Like rain on stone. Like arrows that can't pierce.

Think about what that would mean for your relationships. Arguments wouldn't spiral into weeks of cold silence. Disappointments wouldn't calcify into bitterness. You could stay tender without being fragile. Strong without being hard.

You might still flip a table when injustice demands it. Jesus did. You might still speak up when truth is on the line. But you wouldn't live with the constant sting of *How dare they?* You wouldn't let every slight become a scar. You'd know when anger is righteous and when it's just your pride talking.

That's the freedom of the unoffendable heart.

And here's the secret: It's not about pretending.

It's not about putting on a mask that says you're tougher than you are. It's not about numbing yourself to pain so you never feel any God-given emotions.

And it's not about brushing off real injustice so you can never be used by God to speak truth to power or stand up for the oppressed.

An unoffendable heart doesn't mean you stop caring. It means you care in the right way.

Jesus cared. He wept at a friend's tomb. He got angry at hypocrisy. He let betrayal pierce Him. But He never let offense define Him. Even hanging on a cross, He prayed, "Father, forgive them, for they know not what they do" (Luke 23:34).

That's the heart He gives you. His Spirit in you means His heart can become your heart.

If you are willing to turn the page and come with me in this book, then by the time you finish, you won't just understand the unoffendable heart; you'll begin to live with one.

You'll forgive quickly.

You'll love freely.

You'll stop bracing for the next spark.

You'll carry peace that outlasts disappointment and courage that rises above rejection.

That's the life waiting for you.

In chapter 1, I'll show you the four chambers of your spiritual heart. Just as your physical heart has four chambers pumping life through your body, these four chambers—expectations, justice, confidence, and memory—determine whether your spiritual life is flowing strong or clogged with offense.

When even one chamber is blocked, the whole heart suffers. But when each one is clear, whole, surrendered to Christ, you will finally walk in the freedom of an unoffendable heart.

part one

the wounded heart

1

the heart of the matter

a call to adventure

He was only 44.

An associate pastor in the Midwestern United States, the kind of man whose gentleness carried more weight than a booming voice ever could. He wasn't the preacher who rattled the rafters, and he certainly never chased applause. He was quieter than that. Steadier. The one who noticed when you missed a Sunday, and followed up. The one who remembered the names of your kids. The one who sat with the grieving long after the casseroles stopped coming.

A husband. A highly devoted father of four. Faithful. Compassionate. A lover of Jesus and His Church.

On the outside, he seemed healthy. Smiling. Still moving through the rhythms of ministry and a happy homelife. The kind of man you'd look at and think, *He's got decades ahead of him.*

But underneath, something wasn't right.

It began with small things. A little shortness of breath climbing the stairs. A heaviness in his chest after preaching. A fatigue that clung, even after rest. At first, he brushed it aside. Ministry is exhausting, right? Everyone gets tired. Four kids at home—of course he felt worn down.

Still, his wife noticed. She saw the way he'd pause at the top of the stairs, catching his breath. She heard the sighs he tried to hide at night, the restless turning in bed. She watched his energy wane in ways that weren't normal for a man his age.

"Something's wrong," she told him.

He shrugged it off, comforted by his wife's care, but unconcerned. "I'm fine. Just need to start exercising again."

But she kept urging, kept pressing, until he finally agreed to see a doctor. Just to be safe.

One appointment led to bloodwork. An EKG. A stress test. He walked the treadmill with wires attached to his chest, nurses watching monitors. He pushed himself harder, but the numbers told the truth. Something was very wrong.

By the end of the day, the diagnosis was clear. His arteries were ninety percent blocked.

Ninety percent.

He wasn't just tired. He wasn't just stressed. He was one breath away from collapse.

The doctors didn't wait. "We're scheduling you for open-heart surgery."

"When?" he asked, knowing he had a busy month ahead and hoping he'd have time to clear up a few obligations. Open-heart surgery was a big deal, and he was in shock, but still thinking of the ministry.

"Today," they said. "If we don't act now, the outcome is inevitable."

Open-heart surgery at 44.

The pastor sat there stunned, his wife's nervous but steady hand gripping his. Four kids at home. A big congregation that trusted him. A life that seemed, from the outside, to be just hitting its stride.

And suddenly, it was obvious how fragile it all was.

Back at the church, word began to spread. "Did you hear? Pastor's in the hospital." People were stunned. Some whispered, "But he looked fine." Others said, "I just saw him last week—he seemed healthy." Nobody would have guessed that a man still faithfully showing up for his flock was, inside, one breath away from collapse.

And isn't that how it goes? On the outside, everything looks normal. On the inside, a hidden blockage threatens the whole system.

That's the thing about the heart.

It doesn't need to fail completely to kill you. It only takes one blockage in the wrong place. You can be ninety percent shut down and still moving through life—still showing up at work, still parenting your kids, still smiling for the crowd.

But collapse is coming.

The body can't thrive when the heart is clogged.

The human heart is a marvel—about the size of your fist, weighing less than a pound, beating 100,000 times in a single day. Roughly 35 million beats in a year. It never clocks out, never takes a vacation. As long as it pumps, you live.

When it stops, you stop.

Inside, the heart is divided into four chambers. On the right side, the atrium gets oxygen-poor blood from the body. The right ventricle sends it to the lungs, where it picks up oxygen. On the left side, the other atrium receives this oxygen-rich blood. The left ventricle then pumps it out strongly enough to reach your fingertips and toes.

In under 60 seconds, blood makes a full circuit through your body. Then it starts again, over and over, until you die.

But if one artery feeding those chambers is blocked, the flow is disrupted.

At first, symptoms are subtle. You might feel a bit tired or short of breath. There may be a heaviness you can't explain. If the blockage remains, the heart weakens. Oxygen levels drop, muscles begin to fail, and eventually the whole body suffers.

The heart doesn't have to stop beating to be failing. It just needs to be blocked.

Doctors call it cardiovascular disease. Patients see it as a wake-up call. Families call it a tragedy when it's discovered too late. Whatever you call it, the truth is clear: Even a small blockage in the wrong place can stop everything.

This isn't just a medical fact; it's a lesson.

The same can happen in your inner life.

Think about it. You may seem fine on the outside. You keep working, parenting, and posting pictures that say *I'm okay.* But inside, something feels wrong. You feel emotionally short of breath. Small things weigh you down. The fatigue doesn't go away.

You might not call it offense, but that's what it is.

Unmet expectations that have never healed.

Wrongs and injustices you keep track of.

Confidence shaken by criticism or neglect.

Old memories you think you have moved past, surfacing in your tone and posture.

These feelings don't just sit quietly. They clog the flow of life through your soul.

Proverbs 4:23 says, "Keep your heart with all vigilance, for from it flow the springs of life." The imagery is powerful. Life flows from the heart. It doesn't trickle; it flows.

But if that flow is blocked, everything suffers.

The symptoms are easier to spot than we admit.

That heaviness around certain people, as if they drain you.

Replaying arguments in your mind, even when the other person has forgotten.

How quickly you bristle at the slightest criticism.

The inner voice that insists *it's not fair*, long after the moment has passed.

These aren't just quirks; they are signs of a blocked heart.

That pastor's doctors acted quickly because ignoring the problem wasn't an option. Spiritually, the same is true for us. Offense doesn't go away on its own. It builds up, hardening like plaque, narrowing the flow until collapse is inevitable.

The Spiritual Heart

That image stuck with me, and through it God gave me a way to describe what happens in the soul. Just as the physical heart has four chambers that must stay open for blood to circulate, so our spiritual lives have four chambers that must stay clear if love, joy, and peace are going to flow.

These spiritual chambers are not literal organs. You won't find them in a medical textbook. But the analogy helps us see what offense does inside us.

The four chambers of the spiritual heart are *expectations*, *justice*, *confidence*, and *memory*. When they are clear, your whole being thrives. Love flows naturally. Forgiveness moves quickly. Joy pulses strongly. You can face disappointment without being undone.

But when even one chamber clogs with offense, everything else is affected.

You might still look fine on the outside. You're still working, still raising your kids, still serving at church.

Yet inside, your heart is short of breath.

And left untreated, collapse is inevitable.

The rest of this chapter will be an overview of these four spiritual chambers. Then we'll go even deeper and unpack them further in the chapters that follow.

The Chamber of Expectations

If offense has a favorite hiding place, it's here.

We all carry expectations, though we rarely say them out loud. We expect a spouse to notice when we've put in the extra effort.

We expect a boss to acknowledge our long hours. We expect friends to check in when life feels heavy. And when they don't, when the call never comes, when the thanks never arrive, something inside us clenches.

It's subtle at first. Just a little sigh, a quiet disappointment. But over time, it piles up like a hidden ledger. A scorecard no one else can see. And soon, every interaction runs through it. Instead of love flowing freely, bitterness circulates.

Jesus warned us about this in Luke 17:1: "Offenses will certainly come" (CSB). It's inevitable. The question isn't whether people will fail us. The question is what those failures do inside us.

For some people, unmet expectations calcify into a silent demand: *You owe me*. For others, they turn into silent withdrawals of affection, respect, or trust. Either way, the heart grows heavy, clogged with what people never delivered.

Unmet expectations may look small on the surface, but left unchecked, they suffocate joy. This chamber alone can leave you gasping for air in your relationships, even while everything looks fine on the outside.

We'll come back to this chamber later, because it deserves an entire chapter of its own. For now, remember that expectations, when blocked, are one of the fastest ways to choke the flow of life through your heart.

The Chamber of Justice

If expectations leave us disappointed, the chamber of justice takes it further. This is the part of your heart that cries out, *That's not fair!*

It's where the sting of betrayal burns hottest. Where a harsh word or a public slight replays over and over in your mind. It's the chamber that bristles when someone twists your motives or drags your reputation through the mud.

And it's not just fairness we want. When justice is blocked, we want payback. The inner dialogue sharpens: *They embarrassed me? I'll embarrass them. They hurt me? I'll make them hurt more.*

That reflex for retaliation feels almost natural, like a muscle memory. But it creates an endless cycle. A spouse snaps, so you snap back. A co-worker undermines you, so you look for ways to undercut that person in return. Soon the whole system is poisoned, not just by the original offense, but by the revenge it provoked.

Scripture is blunt here: "Never avenge yourselves. . . . 'Vengeance is mine, I will repay, says the Lord'" (Romans 12:19). God warns us because He knows how easily the chamber of justice clogs. Once it does, the offense doesn't heal; it multiplies.

And that's the danger. This chamber, when blocked, doesn't just weigh you down; it tears communities apart. Families fracture. Friendships die. Churches split. Justice left in our hands turns into retaliation, and retaliation never satisfies.

In a chapter ahead, we'll take time to open this chamber fully. But for now, it's enough to see the danger: When offense clogs the chamber of justice, bitterness and vengeance flood the bloodstream, and the whole heart suffers.

The Chamber of Confidence

The third chamber of the heart is confidence. At its best, this is where trust beats strongly—trust in God, trust in your calling, trust that your worth is not on trial with every passing opinion. But when this chamber is clogged with offense, confidence falters.

It often starts with a single word. A critique that cuts too deep. A mentor who questions your motives. A friend who mocks your faith. Suddenly, your assurance wavers. You replay the moment again and again, not just hearing what was said, but letting it echo into your identity.

The chamber of confidence is especially vulnerable because offense here feels personal. It doesn't just say, *They don't like what I did*. It whispers, *They don't like who I am*.

I've seen this play out in young leaders. One harsh comment from someone they respected, and their whole posture changes. They withdraw. They second-guess every decision. Instead of leading with freedom, they become paralyzed, constantly looking over their shoulder, desperate not to offend again.

And it's not just leaders. It's students who stop raising their hands in class because they were laughed at once. It's employees who stop offering ideas after a single rejection. It's spouses who stop expressing affection because they fear it won't be reciprocated.

The chamber of confidence is where offense attacks our core sense of security. Left unchecked, offense makes us timid, overly cautious, afraid to step into the life God has called us to live.

Proverbs 29:25 warns, "The fear of man lays a snare." When our confidence is entangled in what others think, one offense can bind us tighter than chains.

A clogged chamber of confidence doesn't just hurt *you*. It robs those around you of the strength and courage God meant for you to share. A parent unsure of his or her worth struggles to affirm the children. A pastor wounded by criticism grows hesitant to preach with conviction. A believer afraid of rejection hides the very Gospel that could set others free.

We'll return to this chamber in depth later. For now, know this: When offense clogs your confidence, the whole Body of Christ suffers. This chamber, if blocked, will silence your voice long before God ever intended it to be quiet.

The Chamber of Memory

The fourth chamber of the heart is memory. This is where the past lives. Every moment of betrayal, embarrassment, rejection, and loss can settle here like sediment at the bottom of a river.

Memory itself is not the problem. In fact, it's a gift. God designed memory so we could remember His faithfulness, learn from mistakes, and carry wisdom forward. But when offense settles into this chamber, memories stop teaching and start tormenting.

A conversation from ten years ago suddenly feels fresh again. A face, a place, or even a tone of voice can pull you back into a moment you thought was long gone. Your body tightens, your thoughts replay the scene, and the old wound bleeds as if it just happened.

That's what offense does in the chamber of memory. It keeps the past alive in a way God never intended.

Instead of becoming a testimony of what God healed, the memory becomes a prison that quietly shapes how you trust, how you love, and how you respond to people who had nothing to do with the original hurt.

But when this chamber is healed, something powerful happens. The same memories that once produced bitterness become reminders of God's mercy. The past no longer controls you. It becomes part of the story of how God set you free.

We will explore this chamber more fully later. For now, it's enough to recognize that when offense clogs the chamber of memory, the past keeps bleeding into the present, and the heart struggles to move forward.

Jesus: The Unoffendable Heart

Each chamber matters. Each one can clog. Each one can suffocate the flow of love, joy, and peace, if left untreated.

But here's the good news: There is One whose heart was never clogged.

Jesus lived the only truly unoffendable life.

He was betrayed by friends, slandered by enemies, misunderstood by family, mocked by crowds, and crucified by the very people He came to save. And yet, hanging on the cross, His words weren't bitter. He didn't spit curses at His executioners. He looked toward heaven and prayed, "Father, forgive them, for they know not what they do" (Luke 23:34).

Think about that. The soldiers pounding nails through His hands didn't ask for forgiveness. The crowd taunting Him wasn't sorry. His disciples had scattered in fear. And still, His heart flowed with mercy, not offense.

That's what an unoffendable heart looks like.

It doesn't mean Jesus didn't feel pain. He felt it deeply. It doesn't mean He ignored injustice. He confronted it head on. But He never allowed the venom of offense to spread. His expectations were set on the Father, not on people. His justice was entrusted to God, not driven by revenge. His confidence rested in who He was as the beloved Son, not in public approval. And His memory was filled with the Father's voice, not the accusations of His enemies.

This is why He could endure betrayal without becoming bitter, and why He could be wronged without becoming a wrongdoer Himself.

And here's where the hope comes in: The same Christ now lives in you. His Spirit is able to clear what offense has clogged. He doesn't just set an example and say, "Good luck." He says, "Follow Me, and I will make you more like Me."

The work of becoming unoffendable isn't about straining harder; it's about letting His life flow through yours. Can you imagine it?

Waking up free from the weight of grudges.

Walking into work without silently rehearsing old slights.

Loving family members without keeping score.

Facing criticism without crumbling.
Standing against injustice without being poisoned by vengeance.

That's not wishful thinking. That's the life Jesus makes possible.

In the chapters ahead, we will examine each chamber of the heart—the chambers of *expectations*, *justice*, *confidence*, and *memory*. We will look at how offense sneaks in, how it blocks the flow of life, and how Jesus clears the way. By the time we are done, you will see that offense doesn't have to define you. It doesn't have to control you. You really can walk in freedom.

This is the invitation: to live with the kind of heart that looks like His. A heart that can be grieved but not embittered, tested but not hardened, offended but never taken captive by offense.

The sparks will still fly. But the fire won't consume you.

2

expectations

the ledger of disappointment

Let's start this chapter on the chamber of expectations by looking at three lives that were full of expectation and hope . . . until the chamber clogged.

Sarah

Sarah straightened her blouse in the car mirror and whispered a prayer before walking in. She had been lonely for months, aching for community. When the greeter at the door smiled and said, "Welcome, we're so glad you're here," she felt her chest loosen. A woman handed her a coffee, still steaming, and for a brief moment she imagined what it might be like to belong.

During worship her voice cracked on the high notes, but no one seemed to mind. People had their hands raised, some even crying. The pastor preached about hope, and Sarah scribbled in her notebook as if she were taking notes for an exam. On the drive home, she rehearsed the thought again and again: *This is it. These are my people.*

By the third week, she had joined a small group. The first meeting felt awkward but promising. She expected follow-up texts, dinner invitations, someone to notice her. But even when she missed a week because of work travel, the silence was deafening.

No one checked in. A few days later, a woman she had been trying to connect with made a cutting comment. It was probably nothing intentional, but it pierced.

When Sarah attended small group the next week, she left afterward with her smile fixed in place but her insides heavy. *Maybe I was wrong about this place*, she thought as she drove home in the dark. She didn't leave the church immediately. She just stopped expecting much, and started keeping score.

David

David dropped his briefcase just inside the door and loosened his tie. The smell of spaghetti sauce hung in the air, something burnt underneath it. The twins were running in circles, squealing. His youngest had a crayon clenched in her fist and was scribbling on the wall.

His wife barely looked up from the stove. "Can you take over? I'm losing it tonight."

David swallowed the sting and hung his jacket. He wanted to hear, "I see how hard you're working. Thank you for carrying us." Instead, he rolled up his sleeves and started wiping sauce off the counter.

Later that night, when the kids were finally in bed, he sat beside her on the couch. She scrolled on her phone, exhausted. He waited for a word, a glance. Nothing came.

He leaned back, staring at the ceiling. Another tally on the invisible ledger: *Unappreciated.*

It wasn't a blowup. No shouting match. Just the slow accumulation of disappointment. Every unspoken expectation filed away like another unpaid debt.

Michelle

Michelle tapped her pen against the desk as her boss rattled off performance highlights for the year.

"Josh has really stepped up," he said, eyes skimming the review sheet. "Handled those projects so well under pressure. We're lucky to have him."

Michelle forced a smile. Lucky to have him? She was the one who stayed late, who fixed Josh's mistakes, who kept the clients happy. She waited for her name to appear in the litany of praise. It never did.

By the time the meeting ended, she had scribbled circles into her notepad. "Thanks," she said lightly, standing up. Her boss was already on to the next email.

The next week, Michelle still arrived on time. But the spark was gone. She did the work, but the extra mile, the early morning prep, the late-night follow-ups vanished. Inside, the tally marks screamed: *Overlooked. Invisible. Undervalued.*

A Personal Blow

Three lives. Three rooms. Same ache.

They all started with hope and the belief that someone would see, recognize, and meet them halfway. When that didn't happen, it stung. It grew heavy, like a huge debt waiting to be collected.

That's how the chamber of expectations clogs.

I have felt this firsthand. Early in my ministry, I poured everything into a church, serving under a leader I trusted. We dreamed big together—late-night meetings, whiteboards full of plans, prayers that seemed to shake the room. I expected we were going to change our city, to reach people nobody else was reaching. I built my life around that vision.

And then the bottom fell out. The leader I trusted fell into scandal. The dream cracked apart overnight.

I remember standing in the sanctuary the Sunday after, staring at the stage and wondering, *What now?* The faces of the people I had shepherded looked dazed, as if they had all aged years in a weekend.

The echoes of promises unfulfilled filled the atmosphere—louder than any worship song. A church service turned into an unexpected funeral as we collectively laid to rest the idea that "the best is yet to come."

I was so heartbroken, I left ministry for a season. My chamber of expectations wasn't just bruised; it was blocked with rubble. What I thought would be a future full of fruit had turned into ashes.

The Inheritance of Expectations

For many of us, the ledger doesn't start in adulthood. It begins at home.

Before we ever wrote our first résumé or entered our first relationship, we were already carrying invisible math in our hearts. Every sigh, every slammed door, every unmet hug was a number added to the column of what we thought life should give us, but didn't.

Maybe as a child you learned that kids usually expect certain things from their father—protection, affirmation, provision. Yet your own father was absent, or volatile, or simply distracted, and you felt the sting when your expectations were not met. Maybe you had absorbed expectations about the love and care mothers should provide and how they should nurture. Yet your mother carried the weight of her household with silent endurance, perhaps withdrawn or depressed. Your longings for motherly affection and approval often went unmet, which wounded you.

Children are natural theologians. We build our first doctrines of love, trust, and worth not from sermons, but from supper tables, arguments overheard, and whether or not someone came when we cried. We may not have had the words then, but we learned to believe certain equations: *my needs don't matter*, or *if I work hard enough, I'll be safe*, or *affection always has a cost.*

And here's the problem: Those expectations don't dissolve when you grow up.

They hitchhike into every new relationship. You end up looking to your spouse to heal childhood wounds. You expect your boss to notice you the way your parents never did. You put pastors on pedestals, hoping they'll play the role of the father you never had.

But no pastor, no spouse, no friend can hold that weight. They were not designed to. And when they inevitably stumble, it feels like abandonment all over again. The ledger grows longer.

This is why Jesus pointed His disciples to God as Father. Not simply as a metaphor, but as a corrective: "Call no man your father on earth," He said, "for you have one Father, who is in heaven" (Matthew 23:9). God was giving us a new ledger—one based not on the failures of earthly parents, but on His own unchanging character.

The inheritance of expectations is real. But so is the inheritance of grace.

The Social Media Scoreboard

We don't just inherit expectations; we absorb them every time we pull out our phones.

Comparison used to be local. We measured ourselves against classmates, co-workers, and neighbors. Now the scoreboard is global. We carry in our pockets a constant feed of curated lives, highlight reels disguised as reality.

Scroll long enough and you'll hear a sermon, preached without words: *You should have what they have. You deserve more. Look at what you're missing.*

A friend posts vacation photos. You expected to travel by now too, but the budget says otherwise. Tally mark.

Another friend posts a smiling anniversary picture. You expected marriage to look like that—easy, glowing, Instagram worthy. Tally mark.

Someone brags about a new promotion. You expected recognition too, but it never came. Another mark on the ledger.

The algorithms know exactly what they're doing. Outrage and comparison keep you scrolling. The system profits from your disappointment. It's not a neutral tool; it's a mirror angled just enough to distort your reflection, until you start believing you are behind, unloved, or unseen.

It's an offense economy, designed to feed your unmet expectations back to you, until they poison your perspective. And when you take that poisoned ledger back into your real relationships, no one around you can measure up.

But here's the truth Scripture whispers in contrast: "Godliness with contentment is great gain" (1 Timothy 6:6). That verse cuts through the noise of the feed. The scoreboard doesn't get the last word. Contentment does. We'll learn how throughout the course of this book.

But it's no wonder our hearts are sick. We were never meant to run our lives according to likes, followers, or comparison tallies. Our worth was settled long before smartphones existed.

The Slow Drift

The most dangerous thing about unmet expectations is how quietly they work.

It's rarely one blow that topples a marriage, a friendship, or a church relationship. It's the slow drift.

A husband checks out emotionally because she "doesn't get me."

A wife numbs herself with busyness because he "doesn't notice."

A church member slips from the front row to the back, and then out the door, because "nobody cares."

A son stops returning calls, because every conversation feels like another reminder of how he has failed to live up to expectations.

No explosions. Just slow suffocation. And by the time anyone realizes it, the chamber is almost completely blocked.

History's Harshest Lesson

It isn't only marriages and friendships that collapse under unmet expectations. Sometimes whole lives, whole generations, are crushed by them.

Viktor Frankl, a psychiatrist and a Holocaust survivor, wrote of men in the concentration camps who tied their survival to a date. "We'll be home by Christmas," some said. Others looked to spring, convinced the war would be over by then.

But when those dates came and went and nothing changed, many gave up the will to live. Their bodies followed their hearts. Frankl observed that it wasn't always the starvation or the beatings that killed first. It was the collapse of expectation. The deferred hope made the heart sick, and the sick heart gave up (see Proverbs 13:12). Here's how he put it in his book *Man's Search for Meaning*:

> A man who let himself decline . . . found himself occupied with retrospective thoughts. In a different connection, we once heard a man say that the war would be over on March 30. On March 29 he suddenly became ill and lost consciousness. On March 31, he was dead. To all outward appearances, he had died of typhus. Those who know how close the connection is between the state of mind of a man—his courage and hope, or lack of them—and the state of immunity of his body will understand this death. The ultimate cause of my friend's death was that the expected liberation did not come, and he was severely disappointed. This suddenly lowered his body's resistance against the latent typhus infection. His faith in the future and his will to live had become paralyzed, and his body fell victim to illness—and thus the man died.[1]

"The expected liberation did not come," and his body gave up. That is the ultimate consequence of a blocked chamber. Expectations, left unmet, don't just bruise the soul. They can hollow it out until nothing is left and sometimes even the body gives up.

The Biblical Echo

The destructive power of a blocked chamber of expectations isn't just modern psychology; it's as old as Scripture.

The disciples carried their own ledgers. They expected Jesus to topple Rome, to establish a kingdom on their terms. But instead of rallying an army, He washed their feet. Instead of charging into the palace, He rode a donkey into Jerusalem and surrendered to people's abuse, accusations, and the cross.

The disciples' expectations collapsed, and with them their courage. Peter, the boldest of them all, denied even knowing Jesus, and when the resurrected Christ came looking for them, they had all but given up already.

And then there's John the Baptist.

Think about it: This was the man who pointed at Jesus and declared, "Behold, the Lamb of God, who takes away the sin of the world!" (John 1:29). He had baptized Jesus in the Jordan River, seen the heavens open, and heard the voice of God affirming His Son. If anyone should have had unshakable certainty, it was John.

But prison changes your perspective. Isolated, hungry, cut off from ministry and momentum, John began to question. His expectations of the Messiah included fire and winnowing forks, judgment and vindication. But months passed, and Jesus didn't overthrow the oppressors. Instead, He wandered Galilee healing the sick, eating with tax collectors, and telling cryptic parables.

So John sent his disciples with a heartbreaking question: "Are you the one who is to come, or shall we look for another?" (Matthew 11:3).

Even John, the bold preacher in the wilderness, the forerunner, the prophet, found himself stumbling over unmet expectations. Expectations can choke even the strongest faith. When they do, the heart begins to shut down. John hadn't misunderstood who Jesus was; he had misunderstood how Jesus would work.

Yet Jesus didn't shame John for asking.

He didn't thunder judgment or dismiss John's doubts. Instead, He sent back evidence: "Go and tell John what you hear and see: the blind receive their sight and the lame walk, lepers are cleansed and the deaf hear, and the dead are raised up, and the poor have good news preached to them." (Matthew 11:4–5).

Jesus reframed John's expectations with reality. He was fulfilling the prophecies, but not in the way John anticipated. And then He added this gentle beatitude: "Blessed is the one who is not offended by me" (verse 6).

If John the Baptist could wrestle with unmet expectations, then so can we. And if Jesus had compassion for John, He has compassion for you too.

Taking Inventory to Name the Weight

By now, you might already feel a tug in your chest. Maybe Sarah's story sounds too familiar. Maybe you have lived David's late-night resentment or Michelle's job invisibility. Maybe your own list of unmet expectations is long and raw.

Maybe you have even questioned if Jesus is really the Messiah. After all, wouldn't He be fixing everything if He were?

This is where you pause. Not to fix it. That will come later. But to name the weight on your chest. Ask yourself:

Where have I felt let down recently?

Against whom am I silently keeping score?

What do I wish they would say or do that they haven't?

Don't defend your answers. Don't justify them. Just name them. Even justified expectations, if left unspoken and unmet, can harden into bitterness.

If it helps, write the answers to these questions down. Picture the ledger you've been keeping in your heart. Who is on it? What are the tallies? How heavy has it gotten?

This is your fire drill. Jesus warned us plainly: "Offenses will certainly come" (Luke 17:1 CSB). If you expect the alarm to sound, you won't panic when it does. You'll know how to move.

The Loudest Cry

So let's be honest: This chamber of expectations is clogged in almost all of us.

You can feel it in your own life. The disappointment that still aches years later. The silent resentment that creeps up in marriage. The cynicism about church or work. The fatigue of scrolling through other people's lives, wondering why your life feels smaller.

Every tally mark on the invisible ledger makes it harder for love to flow, harder for joy to rise, harder for hope to take root. And unless something changes, the heart will keep growing heavier, until it stops beating freely.

The truth is that what begins in expectations never stays there. When you've kept score long enough, when the tallies have piled up, the next thing out of your mouth is almost always the same: "It's not fair!"

That cry for justice rises up from the second chamber of the heart, and it may be the loudest one of all.

3

justice

why your heart keeps score

The only perfect man who ever lived stood bound before the religious council. He had healed the sick, raised the dead, fed the hungry, and preached the Kingdom of God. His only "crime" was revealing the truth.

The high priest tore his robes and shouted, "He has uttered blasphemy. What further witnesses do we need?" (Matthew 26:65). Those present demanded, "Prophesy to us, you Christ! Who is it that struck you?" (verse 68).

They spit in His face. They struck Him with their fists. Others slapped Him and mocked. The Roman soldiers then took Him into the governor's headquarters as a whole battalion gathered to watch the sport. They stripped Him naked, draped a scarlet robe over His shoulders, and jammed a crown of thorns into His scalp. Blood streamed down His forehead as they knelt in mock worship, jeering, "Hail, King of the Jews!" (Matthew 27:29). Then they spat on Him again and struck Him on the head with a reed.

This was the most grotesque miscarriage of justice in human history. The One named Justice will return to separate the sheep from the goats. He will "judge the living and the dead" (2 Timothy 4:1). Yet He was condemned by corrupt men. Innocence was declared guilty. Holiness was branded blasphemy. Love was beaten, mocked, and despised.

Do you feel it when you read the Scriptures? That burning in your chest, that cry in your spirit: *This is not right!* Do you feel anger and a desire to make things right by punishing whoever is guilty? That is the chamber of justice responding to the outrage. God put it there. He is "a God of justice" (Isaiah 30:18), and we bear His image.

Writers of books, movies, and plays know this about us. They know we have a built-in sense of justice, so they tell stories about injustice and build a hunger in us for revenge. Then the best stories feed that hunger.

We love watching wrongs get made right, or at least our version of "right." Think of *Gladiator*, where a betrayed general fights his way back to avenge his murdered family and emperor. Or *The Count of Monte Cristo*, where a man wrongfully imprisoned returns years later to bring poetic justice to every betrayer. Even the quieter stories like *Taken*, *John Wick*, or *Kill Bill* work the same way. Someone is wronged, someone suffers, and then someone pays. Those stories stir something in us because they mirror a true and holy longing—the desire for things to be made right.

But that's also what makes such stories dangerous. They satisfy that hunger by feeding us vengeance disguised as justice. We leave the theater cheering not for righteousness restored, but for retribution achieved. We are moved not by mercy, but by mayhem. Our culture calls that catharsis. Scripture calls it wrath.

And it's easy to see why we confuse the two. When we watch the villain fall or the betrayer get exposed, it feels right because it echoes God's design for justice. Yet in the stories we love most, justice almost always comes through violence, deception, or domination, the very tools that keep evil alive.

That's where Jesus breaks the pattern. The only truly innocent man in history stood before His accusers and refused to play the revenge game. "When he was reviled, he did not revile in return; when he suffered, he did not threaten, but continued entrusting himself to him who judges justly" (1 Peter 2:23).

In other words, Jesus did not feed the world's thirst for vengeance. He absorbed it. He did not demand repayment. He became the payment. The very moment we would have drawn the sword, He stretched out His hands.

We cheer for gladiators, avengers, and vigilantes because they act out what we secretly wish we could do. Heaven cheers for the Lamb who was slain, because He acted out what only God could do.

The Foundation of His Throne

Psalm 89:14 says, "Righteousness and justice are the foundation of your throne; steadfast love and faithfulness go before you."

The line isn't just poetic. The psalmist, although likely not David here, points to something deeper. He calls it the structure under everything. It is the moral foundation that guides God's governance of the world.

Every kingdom, divine or human, rises or falls based on what supports it. The biblical text suggests God's reign is unshakable because it rests on righteousness and justice. These aren't just abstract ideas; they describe who God is and how He acts in creation.

The Hebrew word for justice, *mishpat*, means ruling or verdict.[1] It refers to setting things right according to God's righteous standards. This concept shows up over four hundred times in the Old Testament. It highlights the importance of justice in the biblical story. In Deuteronomy 10:18, God "executes justice for the fatherless and the widow, and loves the sojourner, giving him food and clothing." In Isaiah 1:17, He calls His people to "learn to do good; seek justice, correct oppression; bring justice to the fatherless, plead the widow's cause."

Mishpat isn't just about punishing the guilty. It's also about defending those who can't defend themselves and fixing what power has twisted. It's active, not theoretical. Each time someone stands up for a victim, tells the truth at a cost, or exposes a lie, we see God's justice in action. Human courts can be swayed or silenced, but God's justice remains steady. It quietly straightens what pride and fear have warped. When you see true justice, you see God at work.

If *mishpat* is the verdict, then *tsedeq*, or righteousness, is the standard for that verdict. This word means straight or right.[2] It describes a balanced scale, a clear path, a life aligned with holiness. Abraham's question in Genesis 18:25 still resonates: "Shall not the Judge of all the earth do what is just?"

Without *tsedeq*, justice can become cruel. We see this in systems that use law to harm instead of to heal. Without justice, righteousness can become weak, just empty words that don't matter. The two must go together. *Mishpat* and *tsedeq* form the foundation beneath God's throne, the solid ground of His reign. Perhaps that's why His judgments, unlike ours, are fair and final. They set things right in a way we cannot.

A Different Vengeance

Paul writes in Romans 12:19, "Never avenge yourselves, but leave it to the wrath of God, for it is written, 'Vengeance is mine, I will repay, says the Lord.'"

The Greek word Paul uses for vengeance, *ekdikēsis*, literally means justice carried out.[3] Rather than condemn the desire for justice, Paul warns about the danger of making that desire personal. Wanting to make things right is godly. It's a good desire. But in the hands of humans, anger seeps in, pride takes over, fear gets involved, and there is no longer purity in the desire. Justice turns to revenge.

In our hands, we will misjudge the size of a wound. We may punish too harshly. We may not punish enough. We take our pain and we "pay it forward," thinking it will somehow balance the scales. It never does.

God's vengeance is different. It is not emotional or impulsive.

His vengeance is perfect. It's clean, it's holy, and it's final. He adds nothing extra, and He leaves nothing undone.

If you want to see the kind of disaster that can happen when men take on God's job on the earth, keep reading.

This story starts with a pig.

Along the Tug Fork River between the hills of Kentucky and West Virginia, two families lived within earshot of each other: the Hatfields and the McCoys.

These were mountain people. They were tough, proud, and deeply tied to both their land and their name. Honor was not a luxury in that world; it was survival.

Sometime in the 1870s, Randolph "Ran'l" McCoy accused Floyd Hatfield of stealing one of his hogs.

Though the animal had a distinctive notch in its ear, both men swore it was theirs.

The argument ended up in court, presided over by Anderson "Preacher Anse" Hatfield. Notice the last name. This was not a good start.

The small room filled with neighbors who leaned forward hungrily for every word. When the verdict came down in favor of the judge's relative, Floyd Hatfield, the McCoys walked out burning with humiliation and a fierce feeling of injustice, which perhaps was not unfounded.

That single ruling lit a fuse. A minor dispute grew into one of the most infamous feuds in American history.

Years of bloodshed, revenge, and loss ensued, each side convinced they were standing up for justice. Yet they were blinded by pride, fear, and an overfunctioning sense of honor. By the end of the sad saga, both families were devastated and scarred, and no one could even remember what it would have looked like to win. Only the annihilation of the other side would do in the end.

It would take decades for the smoke to clear along the Tug Fork River.

The killings slowed, and then finally, they stopped. There were trials, hangings, prison sentences, and many a mother on both sides burying her sons.

Ellison "Cottontop" Mounts, a member of the Hatfield clan, was hanged in 1890 for his part in the violence, and the same rope pulled down the curtain on the bloodshed.

Happily, in 2003, the descendants of the Hatfields and McCoys, who still lived across the water from one another, gathered together in peace on the very ground that once drank up the blood of their ancestors. If there was any forgiveness still needed, it was given that day among laughter, photographs, and camaraderie at being a part of history.

The lesson endures as a scar on the land. When pride replaces mercy, everyone bleeds. When men take God's vengeance into their own hands, Satan wins and blood flows.

Feuds don't always become a family war, but we have all felt that heat rise when someone wrongs us and we replay the scene in our beds, imagining what we might say or do to even the score. This is precisely where Paul's words become a scalpel in the hands of the Holy Spirit: "Never avenge yourselves, but leave it to the wrath of God, for it is written, 'Vengeance is mine, I will repay, says the Lord.'"

Paul is not just calling us to restraint, but to trust. To believe that God sees every injustice and will deal with it rightly, in His time.

When we hand vengeance back to God, we are not pretending the wrong never happened. We are admitting that only perfect hands can make perfect justice.

God gives us laws and courts because of His mercy for a world that has been trying to destroy itself since Cain killed his brother. Romans 13:3–4 says, "For rulers are not a terror to good conduct, but to bad. . . . For he is the servant of God, an avenger who carries out God's wrath on the wrongdoer."

Judges and courts are God's tools for restraint, reflecting His desire to hold back evil and protect the innocent. The strong would prey on the weak, and chaos would reign where law is absent or corrupt.

God appoints rulers and courts to deliver justice on His behalf, so that the burden of judgment doesn't fall on every wounded soul. The law can't heal the human heart, but it can restrain the chaos that sin unleashes.

Even then, human justice has limits. Courts can punish but cannot purify. They can restore order but not peace. That's why God says, "Vengeance is mine" (Romans 12:19). He doesn't ask you to balance every scale or right every wrong. He lifts that weight from your hands and carries it Himself.

When Justice Becomes Vengeance

The Bible itself gives us sobering examples of what happens when people seize the gavel of justice for themselves. One of the clearest is the story of Jacob's daughter, Dinah.

Genesis 34 tells us that Dinah, the daughter of Leah, went out to visit the women of the land. There she encountered Shechem, the son of Hamor the Hivite. He saw her, seized her, and violated her. It was a shameful act, and Dinah's brothers were rightly outraged. The chamber of justice inside them cried out, *This is not right!*

At first, Shechem sought to make amends in his own way. He spoke tenderly to Dinah afterward and told his father, Hamor, "Get me this girl for my wife" (Genesis 34:4). When Jacob's sons heard the news, they were very angry. They felt indignant because

Shechem had done something outrageous in Israel. He had lain with Jacob's daughter, and that was unacceptable (see verse 7).

The brothers' anger was justified. What had been done was evil. But what they did with their anger crossed the line from justice into sinful vengeance.

The sons of Jacob first spoke deceitfully, demanding that every male in the Hivite city be circumcised before Dinah's family would agree to the marriage. Hamor and Shechem hungrily agreed.

Then Scripture says that on the third day, while every man was still in pain from the circumcision, Dinah's two brothers Simeon and Levi attacked, slaughtering every male with the sword. They killed Hamor, Shechem, and all the other men, and then carried off the women, children, livestock, and everything of value.

What began as outrage at one man's crime ended in the slaughter of an entire city.

Jacob's reaction was telling. He did not praise his sons for defending Dinah's honor. He rebuked them, saying, "You have brought trouble on me by making me stink to the inhabitants of the land" (Genesis 34:30). In other words, they had brought shame and danger upon God's people by their overreach.

This would come back to haunt these two vengeful brothers decades later, when Jacob cursed them on his deathbed:

> Simeon and Levi are brothers—their swords are weapons of violence. Let me not enter their council, let me not join their assembly, for they have killed men in their anger and hamstrung oxen as they pleased. Cursed be their anger, so fierce, and their fury, so cruel! I will scatter them in Jacob and disperse them in Israel.
>
> Genesis 49:5–7 NIV

When we take justice into our own hands, we rarely stop at what is right. The flesh pushes us further. Anger fuels us beyond the original offense. We justify cruelty in the name of justice.

And in the end, we bring reproach on ourselves and on the name of God.

Joseph: The Alternative Path

In a later chapter we will allow Jesus, the Great Physician, access to our own hearts. We will let Him open us up and find our own vengeful feelings of hate, fear, and anger. But for now, I want to show you a biblical example of someone who trusted the Lord.

If Simeon and Levi show us what happens when vengeance rules, Joseph shows us what happens when justice is entrusted to God.

Joseph's story begins with unfairness. His father, Jacob, loved him more than any of his brothers, and that love made his siblings hate him. In some ways, you start out feeling bad for them. Jacob caused problems by his obvious favoritism. But what started as jealousy turned into cruelty. This is actually an understatement. The brothers gave vent to their hatred in the kind of injustice that makes the reader angry.

Seeing Joseph coming toward them in the distance, his brothers cooked up an evil plan. Imagine his surprise when, upon greeting his flesh and blood, he found himself under attack. They seized him, stripped him of his robe, and threw him into a pit. In a last-minute act of mercy, instead of killing him they sold him to passing traders. To cover their evil, they dipped his robe in a goat's blood and brought it to their father, Jacob, pretending that Joseph must have been eaten (see Genesis 37). He had been eaten, but not by a lion—by the hatred of his brothers.

Joseph was sold to an Egyptian official named Potiphar, and things began to go well, because, as the Bible repeatedly reminds us, God was with Joseph, even in his trials.

But then, injustice struck again. After Joseph proved himself faithful in Potiphar's house, the man's wife accused him of sexual assault, though he had done nothing wrong. She had repeatedly attempted to entice him to "lie with" her, and he had righteously refused (Genesis 39:7). Then, when she tried again, Joseph fled the house, but left behind part of his clothing in her grasp. She pounced on the moment, taking out the vengeance of her scorned heart by lying about the situation.

Her lie landed Joseph in prison, alone. He had gone from favored son to enslaved servant to condemned prisoner. Joseph's heart must have cried out again and again, *This is not fair!* He was forgotten by everyone except God.

Here's where the story takes a turn. Joseph had every reason to become bitter, to plot revenge, to give up on God altogether. Yet he didn't. He chose trust over retaliation. He chose to surrender and make the most of his situation. Later, after he helped Pharaoh's chief cupbearer, also a prisoner, he was once again forgotten in prison (see Genesis 40). But still, he did not scheme for a way out.

Finally, God gave him his moment. Pharaoh had a troubling dream. God gave Joseph the interpretation and the wisdom to use his new position to serve rather than to settle old scores.

And then came the moment of truth.

Standing face-to-face with the very brothers who had betrayed him, Joseph held all the power to crush them. They would have deserved it. Joseph could have ordered their deaths or enslaved them in return for selling him into slavery. Either would have been fair.

Instead, Joseph broke down in tears. He embraced his brothers. And eventually he said words that have carried through generations: "You meant evil against me, but God meant it for good, to bring it about that many people should be kept alive" (Genesis 50:20).

Joseph did not pretend the wrong never happened. He called it what it was. Evil.

But Joseph trusted God and refused to carry vengeance in his heart. He had learned to recognize God's hand working beyond the limits of his own pain. By trusting God with justice, Joseph was set free from bitterness and was able to see the big picture. God used him to save nations, which could not have happened without the calamity he had endured.

That's the choice Scripture holds up before us. Simeon and Levi answered injustice with violence, and their anger spread destruction. Joseph chose to trust God instead, and his trust brought life.

My Journey Through a Diseased Chamber

I know what it is to have the chamber of justice sick with offense. Nearly twenty years ago, as I described earlier, I learned my pastor had fallen into sin. Infidelity. A whole church unraveling. I had just begun in ministry, and my expectations of what God was going to do through us collapsed overnight.

At the same time, my biological father died, a man I never truly knew. In one season, both spiritual and natural fathers were gone. My heart cried out, *God, this is not fair! I did the right things. I sacrificed. I obeyed. Where is justice?*

Instead of entrusting my pain to the Lord, I picked up the gavel. I began calling out pastors publicly. Online, in conversations, in my own spirit, I made myself the arbiter of right and wrong. I developed a dark persona. People even nicknamed me Johnny Cash, because they never knew if I would sing a gospel song or punch someone in the face.

I thought I was standing for righteousness, but in truth I was feeding a diseased chamber of justice. Offense was rotting me from the inside. I stepped out of ministry. I drowned my bitterness in alcohol. I was determined to vindicate myself and set the record straight, and in doing so, I nearly destroyed my calling.

But God, in His mercy, led me to Jericho. Like David's humiliated men who were told to wait until their beards grew back (see 2 Samuel 10:5), I had to retreat to the sweet place. I deleted my social media accounts. I stepped away from the spotlight. I let God regrow what offense had stripped away. Slowly, painfully, He restored my honor, my identity, and my authority.

Years later, He gave back the things I had surrendered to offense. My influence grew again, but this time I spoke from a healed justice chamber. I no longer needed to expose or retaliate. I spoke with the heart of the Father. What the enemy meant for harm, God turned for good.

Justice, Not Revenge

History shows us that the difference between justice and vengeance is the difference between life and death, renewal and ruin.

Many revolutions began with a legitimate cry for justice, but then descended into rivers of blood because that cry was twisted into vengeance.

The French Revolution is the perfect example. Anyone who reads about the feudal systems of European monarchies will understand the desire of the underclasses for justice. In a society where you have very few rights, resentment will eventually reach a boiling point. Mankind in those days took to heart the admittedly biblical idea that God ruled through divinely ordained kings and queens, who ruled lords, who ruled peasants, who ruled slaves. It was seen as the godly order of things. But since kings, queens, and lords are sinful humans, injustices have pervaded every human kingdom that ever existed. Those injustices supposedly received divine support. No wonder the lower classes cried for revolution.

The French Revolution in the late 1700s began with a plea for liberty from oppression, but quickly turned into an orgy of blood and revenge. The guillotine became the symbol of "justice." One wave of executions led to another, until the streets of Paris ran red with blood. Yes, tyranny was torn down, but it was only replaced by terror. Human wrath multiplied misery. Napoleon crowned himself emperor, and the cycle continued.

The same pattern has appeared in countless uprisings. What begins as a noble longing for freedom often collapses into cycles of violence because people take into their own hands what belongs to God alone. Vengeance never heals. It only spreads the wound wider.

I'm not saying men and women should never stand against injustice. In contrast to many, Martin Luther King Jr. stood before a nation that was seething with racial injustice. Lynchings, segregated schools, economic exclusion, and daily humiliation pressed heavily on the Black community in America.

The chamber of justice in millions cried out, *This is not right!* But King did something novel, having been inspired by his study of Mahatma Gandhi's nonviolent resistance, and by his own pilgrimage to India in 1959. Rather than calling his followers to rise in violence, King thundered the words of the prophet Amos: "Let justice roll down like waters, and righteousness like an ever-flowing stream" (Amos 5:24).

King's cry was not the cry of vengeance, but of Christlike justice.

He chose the cross-shaped path of nonviolence. He refused to pick up the sword of revenge and used his influence to urge people not to return hatred with hatred, but to overcome evil with good. He preached, "Darkness cannot drive out darkness; only light can do that. Hate cannot drive out hate; only love can do that."[4]

Because Martin Luther King Jr. entrusted vengeance to God, his movement did not collapse into terror.

Instead, his voice still calls nations to this day to repentance and hope. Like Joseph, King absorbed injustice without returning it in kind. Like Christ, he chose to bear the wound rather than pass it on.

That is justice without vengeance. That is righteousness rolling down like a mighty river.

An even greater stage revealed the same principle. If you really want to get your blood boiling, read about apartheid South Africa.

Law is supposed to be the God-ordained protection from human oppression, but in this case, it was the blunt weapon used to strip Black South Africans of land, rights, and dignity.

Families were driven from their homes at gunpoint, children beaten for simply speaking their native African tongue. Humans were imprisoned without trial, tortured to get false confessions, and executed wrongly.

By the grace of God, apartheid finally crumbled, and the courts were filled with stories that would break your heart. The Truth and Reconciliation Commission opened its doors, and wave after wave of victims stepped forward to speak.

Mothers told of sons who disappeared in the night when they were taken by security forces, never to return. These mothers described the knock at the door, the sound of boots, the silence that followed, and the years of waiting for bodies that never came home. Fathers recounted being forced to watch while bulldozers leveled the homes of their families, their children standing in the dust of everything they owned.

Entire communities testified to being herded onto trucks and driven miles away from ancestral land so their neighborhoods could be handed over to white settlers. Workers told how they were beaten and jailed for striking, students how they were gunned down for protesting. Survivors recounted electric shocks, suffocation, and brutal torture inflicted in the name of "law and order."

One mother stood in court and described how police handed her the charred remains of her son in a box, his body burned beyond recognition. Another man described watching friends dragged into cells, hearing their screams through the night, and never seeing them again.

The chamber of justice in almost every human heart cried out, *This was not right!*

The sheer weight of the testimony shook the conscience of a nation. It would have been natural for rage to boil over, for blood to answer blood, for revenge to drown the land in violence. South Africa stood on the edge of a fire that could have consumed it whole.

And then came Nelson Mandela. After his 27 years in prison, no one would have blamed him for unleashing fury when he ascended to the presidency. He had every reason to call for vengeance, every excuse to let wrath burn. Instead, he called for forgiveness. He insisted on reconciliation. He invited both victim and perpetrator to step into the light of truth—not to excuse sin, but to confess it and move forward.

Mandela understood what few leaders do: Vengeance multiplies wounds, but justice entrusted to God can heal a nation. South Africa did not descend into civil war. Instead, it found a fragile but real peace, because one man refused to pick up the sword of revenge.

Mandela's choice echoed the same path Joseph had walked centuries earlier. Joseph stood before the brothers who betrayed him, power in his hands to destroy them. Instead of enacting vengeance, he wept and declared, "You meant evil against me, but God meant it for good" (Genesis 50:20). Mandela, too, stood before the perpetrators of unspeakable evil. Instead of answering cruelty with cruelty, he extended forgiveness. Both men show us what happens when the chamber of justice is placed in God's hands rather than our own.

And yet Joseph, Mandela, and Martin Luther King Jr. were only shadows of a greater One. Jesus Christ bore the weight of the greatest injustice in history. The sinless Son of God was condemned as a criminal, beaten, mocked, and nailed to a cross because of Adam's sin, and even yours and mine. From the cross, with every reason to call down vengeance from heaven, He instead prayed, "Father, forgive them, for they know not what they do" (Luke 23:34).

This is the way of God's justice: Joseph forgives his brothers, Mandela forgives his captors, Christ forgives His executioners. Each refuses to let vengeance rule. Each entrusts judgment to the One who judges rightly. Each shows us that true justice is not the work of human wrath, but of divine mercy.

A Glimpse Ahead

For now, pause. Sit with what has been uncovered in your own chamber of justice. Ask yourself:

Where do I feel the searing heat of unfairness?

Where do old wounds still fester in me and cry out for justice?

Where do I still feel the longing for vengeance?

Ask God to shine His light into those places. We will come back to this later, I promise.

Resist the urge to rush toward solutions or answers. This is the searching work of the Spirit. Whatever you normally do to console yourself and forget what lies beneath the surface, don't.

In the chapters ahead, we will begin to look upward. We will see how God Himself brings healing, help, and change. We will learn what it means to become unoffendable, like our Lord, who was mocked, beaten, and condemned, yet never picked up the gavel of vengeance.

Let the Spirit search you. Let Him show you what still lingers in your heart's chamber of justice. Only then will you be ready for the freedom that lies ahead.

Only when every spiritual chamber has been searched will we be ready to discover how God heals and transforms the offended heart. That journey continues in the next chapter, with the chamber of confidence.

4

confidence

the fear of people's opinions

My wife, Julie, kept a secret from me for years. It was bound in leather, hidden on a shelf, and filled with words that recorded my failures.

We had married young. I was only 22 and brought into the marriage a heart scarred by divorce, addiction, and anger. I had no model for healthy love. Julie, who processed life by writing, began to keep a journal. But along with prayers and dreams, she documented in detail all my failures.

Every sharp word I spoke in frustration. Every lapse in self-control. Every disappointment that left her feeling alone. She wrote it all down. Page after page became a silent record of wrongs, a ledger of wounds. Not to be read by the world, but to stand as proof that what she endured was real. Proof that she had been wronged and survived. Proof that I really was as bad as I believed deep down.

Julie had every right to those records. They were the evidence of what she endured. She had become the unintentional casualty of my personal woundedness. She didn't deserve it. I never married her with the intention of hurting her, but I became my own father through another path. Satan has a way of getting us to the same broken ancestral destination from a different route. I swore

I would never treat my wife the way my father had treated my mother, and yet there I was, repeating the cycle.

That journal was both shield and shackle. For Julie, it was a way of coping. For me, it eventually became a mirror. When I learned about it, I felt exposed. My worst fear was confirmed: Someone really was keeping score. Someone was measuring me against the standard of who she thought I should be, and I was failing.

That's what fearing others feels like. It's like living under constant watch, fearing a negative judgment. Even if no one writes down your mistakes, it feels as if a silent witness records every flaw.

Julie's journal was real, but most of us carry these records in our minds. They exist in our family's faces, our co-workers' expectations, and social media posts. This snare isn't just outside; it digs deep into our hearts. You start to think someone is always judging you, making his or her opinion more important than God's.

Proverbs 29:25 states, "The fear of man lays a snare, but whoever trusts in the Lord is safe." The Hebrew word for fear is *pachad*, which means dread or terror before others' power.[1] It's not about respect; it's intimidation. The word for snare is *moqesh*, like a trap set with hidden ropes.[2] The image is clear: Fear of others lurks unseen, waiting to catch you off guard.

This isn't just poetry; it's science. Psychologists call it *social conformity*. God wired our brains with mirror neurons that react to other people's responses. The same brain areas that feel physical pain also react to social rejection.

In other words, disapproval hurts. Seeking approval may feel like a balm, water to a thirsty man in the desert and the only thing that will save, but the fact is that seeking approval makes you a prisoner to the crowd.

The apostle Paul shows that he is not immune to this struggle when he asks, "Am I now seeking the approval of man, or of God?

. . . If I were still trying to please man, I would not be a servant of Christ" (Galatians 1:10).

I wonder what seeking people's approval caused in Paul? Was it pleasing others that had him arresting and killing Christians? The Greek word for please is *areskō*, which means to bend toward someone else's will.[3]

Paul says you can't serve men and Christ at the same time; one will always win.

It's an either/or situation.

John's gospel shows how strong the fear of man can be, even when someone knows what is true. Jesus performed miracles that couldn't be denied. The blind saw, the lame walked, the dead rose, bread and fish appeared out of almost nowhere. The crowds were amazed, as the religious leaders watched.

These leaders scoured the Law and the Prophets, claiming to long for the coming of the Messiah. Yet when He stood before them, they were full of fear, not faith.

The leaders faced the choice we all face: Following Jesus meant opposing the system—the very system that gave them power, and further, gave them their identity.

Confessing Jesus as the Messiah openly risked the loss of everything these men had built their lives on. They would be cut off from the synagogue, the heart of their social and spiritual lives. What would people say?

The price was too high.

John says, "Nevertheless, many even of the authorities believed in him, but for fear of the Pharisees they did not confess it, so that they would not be put out of the synagogue; for they loved the glory that comes from man more than the glory that comes from God" (John 12:42–43).

The Greek word for glory is *doxa*, meaning reputation or honor.[4]

These rulers believed in Christ, but chose silence.

They saw the Light of the world, but feared human judgment to the point that they rejected Him. Men with the spiritual authority to sanction Him recognized the Son of God, but were too afraid to speak His name.

This detail often goes unnoticed because we picture the Pharisees as united in their hatred of Jesus. But some believed, yet buried that belief under social pressure.

They were torn between losing their status and the desire to follow the truth.

This is heartbreaking, and it happens today as well.

Saul: An Old Testament Failure of Confidence

Saul was the first king of Israel.

His story begins with promise, but also a bit of a black mark.

God did not want the Israelites to have a human king. Samuel, the judge of Israel, understood this and knew that God in heaven was their King. Asking for a human king was a serious offense. And yet, though the request came from a heart of rebellion, it also was part of God's ultimate plan.

God's Son would one day arrive as the King of kings and would need to come from the line of kings established in these Old Testament days. Ultimately, Jesus would come from David, of the tribe of Judah. But before David, God had anointed Saul, of the tribe of Benjamin, to be king.

Saul looked every bit the part.

The Bible describes him as "a handsome young man" and says, "There was not a man among the people of Israel more handsome than he. From his shoulders upward he was taller than any of the people" (1 Samuel 9:2). Outwardly, Saul looked like a king with his stature, fighting skill, and presence.

When the prophet Samuel anointed him, Saul was a nobody who was given a fresh start, a chance to lead God's people in righteousness and help them continue their quest to populate the Promised Land they had fought so hard to occupy under Joshua and the judges. But insecurity was already eating him away.

The first public glimpse of Saul's struggle comes at the very beginning of his reign, at his coronation. Samuel gathered the tribes and cast lots to reveal Israel's new king. The lot, by God's hand, fell to Saul, but no one could find him. They went looking for their new king, and the Bible says, "But when they sought him, he could not be found. So they inquired again of the LORD, 'Is there a man still to come?' and the LORD said, 'Behold, he has hidden himself among the baggage'" (1 Samuel 10:21–22).

I don't think the Israelites used the term *baggage* the way we do today, but I wonder if the Holy Spirit understood back then that most of us would know quite well what it feels like to "hide behind our baggage."

What kind of baggage do you hide behind in your quest to avoid the disapproval of other people?!

I know some of mine.

All baggage starts with childhood, maybe in the womb. It says, *You're not enough*.

So we hide.

Imagine Israel's new king, chosen out of seemingly nowhere and anointed by the God of Abraham, hiding among the luggage. He should have been standing tall in front of the people, ready to walk into his calling, his anointing.

Instead, he is crouching in terror behind some baggage.

Some might mistake this for humility. This is not a picture of humility. It's a picture of insecurity. It's the fear of man. Before Saul ever sits on the throne, the snare of approval and the weight of opinion already grip him. This doesn't look good, because if this is how the new king starts, wait until he actually has to make decisions and do something.

This thread of insecurity runs throughout his reign.

At the most critical moments, Saul bends beneath the pressure of other people instead of standing firm in obedience to God.

The most devastating example comes in 1 Samuel 15. Through Samuel, God had commanded Saul to devote the Amalekites and all they possessed to destruction. The Amalekites were pure evil. The whole time the Israelites were struggling through the wilderness, the Amalekites dogged their rear, attacking relentlessly like a pack of hyenas and picking off the weak. God had pronounced His judgment on them and swore to remove them from the earth.

Therefore, His order to King Saul was to leave nothing. No spoil, no compromise, and no partial obedience. But Saul spared the Amalekite king and the best of the livestock.

He simply decided he knew better than God.

Why?

When Samuel arrived, Saul was terrified of what he knew must come next. Samuel confronted Saul, as the animal sounds of obvious disobedience filled the air. Saul proudly announced that he had done the will of the Lord.

Samuel countered, "What then is this bleating of the sheep in my ears and the lowing of the oxen that I hear?" (1 Samuel 15:14).

Saul attempted to cover himself. He claimed that the people had spared the animals for sacrifice.

But Samuel cut through the excuse: "Has the LORD as great delight in burnt offerings and sacrifices, as in obeying the voice of the LORD? Behold, to obey is better than sacrifice, and to listen than the fat of rams" (verse 22).

After some spin and double-talk on Saul's part, Samuel called his bull. Then came Saul's devastating confession: "I have sinned, for I have transgressed the commandment of the LORD and your words, because I feared the people and obeyed their voice" (verse 24).

The Hebrew word for voice is *qōl*. It means more than just spoken words. It can mean influence, proclamation, or command.[5] Saul wasn't simply listening to the people's suggestions. He was submitting to their influence.

The *qōl* of his soldiers carried more weight in Saul's heart than the *dābār*—the word—of his God.[6] That single decision revealed the pattern of his reign. Saul lived bent toward people instead of rooted in obedience to God.

This was not his only stumble.

After David's victory over Goliath and the Israelites' rout of the Philistines, the women of Israel poured into the streets of the city with tambourines and singing. Their voices rose in celebration of national deliverance: "Saul has struck down his thousands, and David his ten thousands" (1 Samuel 18:7).

What should have been a moment of shared triumph became the seed of envy in Saul's heart. Instead of celebrating the young warrior who had rescued Israel, Saul burned with jealousy.

Scripture says, "Saul eyed David from that day on" (verse 9). The chant of the crowd grew louder in his ears than the voice of God. Every cheer for David sounded to Saul like an insult. Every victory David won felt like a loss to him.

Over time, that jealousy hardened into fear.

The man who had once hidden among the baggage to avoid his own coronation now hid behind suspicion and rage. Saul became consumed with defending his own reputation. His fear of being overshadowed poisoned his soul and blinded him to the grace that had first lifted him to the throne.

This part would be comical if it weren't tragic. When we are insecure and crave the approval of others, we build all kinds of monuments to ourselves. We do it by the homes we build, the clothes we wear, the things we brag about on social media. But at Carmel, Saul literally built a monument for himself (1 Samuel 15:12), a desperate attempt to project strength.

It was a great big monument—a victory pillar—erected to display his glory.

But self-promotion is always a fake. It's the counterfeit of confidence. Saul's monument was not an overflow of identity, but a cover for insecurity.

And perhaps the clearest evidence of his failed confidence came with Goliath. When we study that story in Sunday school, we celebrate David. But we don't usually talk about the dark side of this story. Saul was the king and the tallest man in Israel. A proven warrior. He should have been the one to step forward and represent his people against the giant.

Instead, the king sat in his tent, paralyzed for days and days. The king of Israel, chosen to lead God's army, watched as a shepherd boy stepped into the place that should have been his.

Poetic, isn't it?

David would indeed step into Saul's place when he was anointed king instead of Saul. Saul forfeited his calling not because he lacked strength or stature, but because he lacked confidence rooted in God.

The fear of man consumed him, when the fear of God could have emboldened him. He feared the *qōl* of the people more than the *dābār* of the Lord. King Saul feared being overshadowed more than he feared being disobedient.

In the end, his insecurity led to unbelief, and Saul lost his kingdom—not to a stronger army or a more skilled rival, but to the invisible prison of opinion.

His baggage never left him, and he never stopped hiding behind it.

Saul's story stands as one of the clearest warnings in Scripture: The fear of man will always shrink your calling, steal your courage, and ultimately rob you of the future God has placed before you.

Even though Saul was anointed, that anointing was lost by his own fears.

The Fear of Man in All of Us

The sad truth is that we are all more like Saul than we would like to think.

It seems to be a key feature of the human condition ever since the fall of mankind in the Garden (see Genesis 3). Saul's story is not just an ancient tragedy. It is a mirror, if we have the guts to look. The same weakness that snared him still lurks in our own hearts.

The tragic and devastating effects of the fall introduced the fear of man into the human heart. Adam's first failure seems to have been in part fueled by this fear. It was Eve who handed him the fruit. Scripture says simply, "She also gave some to her husband who was with her, and he ate" (Genesis 3:6).

Paul tells his protégé Timothy that Adam was not deceived in the same way Eve was (see 1 Timothy 2:14). Adam knew the command of God, yet he chose silence, and he chose complicity. Is it such a stretch to think that in that moment, Adam feared his wife's disapproval more than he feared disobeying God? The need to please her, the dread of rejection, the desire to keep the peace at any cost—these were at play in the Garden, and they are still at play in us. (I wonder if Eve kept a journal!)

Let's deal with a question this brings up. How could this problem have plagued Adam *before* he fell and corrupted his own nature by his rebellion and disobedience? This is one of the great questions of theology, and it seems to have something to do with the snake. If we didn't already have enough fear, insecurity, and baggage from our upbringing, don't forget the one who hates us and never stops lying. One second before Adam took the bite, he was without sin, and still he succumbed to Satan's influence. What about us, saved, but with sin in the old man, the flesh?

From that day in the Garden forward, humanity has wrestled with the weight of other people's opinions. We are trained in it almost from birth.

For some it begins early, with critical parents. Every action is measured. Every mistake is magnified.

Baggage.

Love feels conditional, and approval becomes the prize to be won rather than a gift freely given.

Baggage.

You learn quickly that if you don't meet the expectations of those who raised you, affection will be withheld. And so the baggage, the fear of other people's opinions, takes root.

The next-level training ground is the classroom. A teacher's harsh words or constant comparisons cut into your heart. A red mark on a paper feels like a verdict on your worth. The fear of failing in front of others zaps your confidence for life, unless God intervenes.

Baggage.

And then there are classmates and neighborhood kids. Children can be cruel, and the playground is often a crucible of conformity. One mocking laugh, one nickname, one rejection by the "in crowd," and you learn to adjust yourself to avoid standing out. Go to the nearest school and you'll see that everyone looks the same, because in that place, you dress to blend in. You do whatever it takes to hide what makes you different. You train yourself to read the room before you dare to speak. But you're never careful enough, and even the most popular kids get plagued by the fear of rejection. There is always someone better, richer, with better clothes, with wealthier parents, smarter, a better athlete. You name it. It doesn't matter what it is. If comparison and judgment are there, the fear of man and the longing for approval are there.

One man I know was like many who, believing they couldn't compete in the contest to be the coolest, became the class clowns. No one respected him, but at least they laughed at his jokes. Who cared that they laughed *at* him as much as they laughed *with* him? But deep down, he hated himself and wished to be someone else. Someone respected and loved.

Baggage.

By the time we reach adulthood, the patterns are well rehearsed and deeply entrenched. We carry the same instincts into our jobs, our marriages. We even take them into our churches and Bible studies. We sit silently in meetings, not because we have nothing to contribute, but because we dread the sting of disapproval. Or we don't sit silent when we should, because we have learned that constantly running our mouth is a way to get desperately needed attention.

We soften our convictions because we don't want to be labeled "too intense" or "too religious" or "too rigid." We laugh at dirty jokes that trouble our conscience, because conformity feels safer than confrontation.

Like Saul, we bend beneath the *qōl*, the voices of others, rather than standing on the *dābār*, the word of God. Like Adam, we choose complicity over courage, silence over truth, Satan over God, fallenness over righteousness.

Simply put, this is the human condition apart from the intervention and sacrificial love of Christ.

The fear of man is not simply a bad habit. It is the echo of Eden and the inheritance of a fallen world, teaching us to measure our lives by other people's faces instead of God's presence. It makes us highly offendable.

The Fear of Man in Our Culture

At its core, the fear of other people's opinions is always about status. It is status seeking in disguise. We crave recognition, belonging, and approval. When our confidence is not anchored in God, we try to manufacture it by securing a place in the eyes of others. This is counterfeit confidence. It looks like strength, but it is really insecurity dressed up in borrowed applause.

The Bible gives us a vivid picture of this counterfeit confidence at work in Saul when he set up that monument for himself at Carmel.

That is the heart of status seeking: making sure others see and admire you, even if your obedience is partial and your heart is insecure.

Today, we build monuments differently. They may look like follower counts, résumés, curated social media feeds, cars and clothes we can't afford, or carefully crafted reputations. But the root is the same. Status seeking is the disease, and tribalism and virtue signaling are two of the most common and damaging ways we pursue it. Let's take a closer look at each of these ways.

Tribalism: status through belonging

Tribalism says, *If I can prove I belong to this group, then I matter.* It offers safety and identity, but at the cost of truth. In a world built around comparison and allegiance, belonging becomes the ultimate badge of worth. We begin to believe that being accepted by the right people will protect us from rejection or insignificance.

This is why John tells us that although many rulers believed in Jesus, "for fear of the Pharisees they did not confess it" (John 12:42). Their standing in the synagogue meant more than their standing before God. They wanted to keep their place at the table, even if it meant turning their backs on the truth.

Tribalism thrives in our day. It shows up in politics when people silence conviction for the sake of party loyalty. It shows up in workplaces when employees look the other way rather than risk being the one who challenges the status quo. It even shows up in churches when culture becomes more powerful than Scripture. We may not bow to carved idols, but we often bow to social ones. In every case, the fear of losing status in the group outweighs the fear of disobeying God. We are living in a cultural moment when the very fabric of society is being pulled apart by this pursuit of belonging at any cost.

Virtue signaling: status through performance

Virtue signaling is another form of counterfeit confidence. It says, *If I say the right things, if I show outrage at the right time, if I appear righteous in public, then I will gain honor*. It feeds on visibility. The more others see our "righteousness," the more secure we feel. Yet Jesus warned, "Beware of practicing your righteousness before other people in order to be seen by them" (Matthew 6:1).

Virtue signaling looks like courage, but it is often fear in disguise. We post our opinions online to make sure we are seen on the "right side of history."

We echo the outrage of the moment so that no one questions our compassion; we shape our words to match the mood of the herd rather than the command of God. This gives the illusion of moral strength, but underneath lies the same old craving for approval. It's not about truth or conviction. It's about managing appearance and protecting reputation.

Whether through virtue signaling or tribalism, the root issue is the same: We are seeking status apart from God. Status seeking is counterfeit confidence because it depends on the shifting sands of opinion rather than the solid foundation of identity in Christ. And it never satisfies. You can always lose your tribe. You can always be outperformed in virtue. You can always be forgotten when the applause moves on.

This is the cycle of the fear of man. It traps us in endless comparison, shallow belonging, and restless striving. It promises safety, but it leaves us empty. Until we see it for what it is, it will continue to shape our chamber of confidence in destructive ways. Only when the fear of others' opinions is replaced by the fear of the Lord will our confidence finally rest on something unshakable.

Reflecting on Your Confidence Chamber

It's easy to read about Saul and think, *Wow, what a mess*. It's a lot harder to admit how much of Saul's problem lives inside us too. Truth is, every one of us has areas where what *other people* think drowns out what *God* says, and it keeps us from being fully obedient to Him.

So let's slow down here and ask ourselves, *Where does the fear of man live in me?*

Don't rush your answer. Pray David's prayer: "Search me, O God, and know my heart! Try me and know my thoughts! And see if there be any grievous way in me, and lead me in the way everlasting!" (Psalm 139:23–24). Then walk slowly through the questions at the end of the following six sections. We're going to invite Jesus to heal these places before this book is done, but right now it's time to take a hard, honest look at your confidence chamber.

Don't rush past these reflections either. Write down what comes up. Let the Holy Spirit put His finger on specific names, situations, conversations. The fear of man *is* a snare, but you can't break free from a trap you won't name. And as you work through all of this, remember the promise we already read (and will read again) in Proverbs 29:25—that "whoever trusts in the LORD is safe."

1. Silence or speech

Think back to the last time you felt the truth burning inside you, but you didn't speak it. Maybe it was in a meeting and something didn't sit right. Maybe your friend needed honesty, but you gave a half-truth instead and told yourself you were "keeping the peace." But deep down, you knew it was fear.

John described some leaders who believed in Jesus but stayed quiet because "they loved the glory that comes from man more than the glory that comes from God" (John 12:43). Ever feel like that? Where has wanting *people's* approval kept you from doing what glorifies *God*?

Take a second. Picture that moment. Ask yourself: *What stopped me? Whose approval mattered more?*

2. Image management

We live in a world obsessed with image. And I'm not just talking about how you dress or how you show up in person. I mean what you post online. How much time do you spend trying to look impressive? Posting the wins, the highlights, the things that make you look good? Or maybe you go the other way—sharing all the chaos and drama to get sympathy and attention. Either way, it's about looking special.

As we saw earlier, Paul said it bluntly: "Am I now seeking the approval of man, or of God? Or am I trying to please man? If I were still trying to please man, I would not be a servant of Christ" (Galatians 1:10). You can't please people and serve Christ. One will always push the other out.

So sit with this: *How do I use social media to try to look special in other people's eyes?*

3. Everyday choices

Fear of other people's opinions doesn't just show up in big betrayals. Most of the time, it sneaks into the small, everyday stuff. You soften what you really believe in a conversation so you don't come off as too intense. You stay quiet about your faith at work because you don't want to be "that person." You go along with plans you know aren't healthy because you don't want to seem difficult.

Proverbs 29:25 says, "The fear of man lays a snare, but whoever trusts in the Lord is safe." A snare is subtle. You don't always see it until you're caught—living a double life, shifting your convictions depending on who's in the room. That's not being flexible. That's being fake.

Ask yourself: *Where am I living for other people's acceptance? What compromises feel small now, but could trap me later? What would happen if I just told the truth instead of what people want to hear?*

4. Deep roots

The fear of man doesn't start when you're an adult. It usually goes back to childhood, maybe even earlier. Even good parents planted some of this when they praised us for everything: "Good job walking! You're amazing!" Sounds harmless, right?

But then add a parent's constant criticism. A teacher's sharp words. Classmates' laughter. Those moments teach you that acceptance is fragile and approval has to be *earned*, no matter what it costs.

Ask yourself: *What early experiences trained me to fear rejection? How are those old wounds still shaping me today? Where do I need God's help to rewrite the script?*

5. Courage check

For some of us, fear of man shows up most when it's time to *act*. You hesitate to pray out loud. You avoid talking about your faith with a friend. You shrink back from speaking hard truth in love, not because you doubt God, but because you're scared of how people will look at you afterward. And that fear overshadows your faith, making it feel weak.

Consider: *Where is fear of what people will think silencing me right now? What would courage look like, even just one small step?*

6. Self-defense

When someone has a problem with you, can you actually *listen*? Can you hear the other person's point and ask yourself if it's true? Or do you immediately start explaining, justifying, defending yourself? When you mess up, can you just say you're sorry, or do you have to explain *why* you did it and why you think that person's feelings are invalid?

Back to Saul. Samuel had to cut through all his excuses before they could get to the real issue.

And watch out for lying. We learn young to lie to protect our image. That's a dead giveaway of the fear of man.

Ask yourself: *When was the last time I heard criticism without jumping straight into self-defense or bending the truth?*

Glimpses of Courage and Confidence

Unless you're a sociopath, you've felt at least some of these signs that the fear of man has set up camp in your heart's chamber of confidence. All of us know what it's like when someone disapproves of us. We've all caught ourselves comparing. We've all felt someone else's opinion sitting on our chest like a weight we just can't shake.

I promise I'll show you where the cure for this lives in later chapters. But right now, I want to show you a few living pictures of what courage, peace, and confidence actually look like. These are examples of what happens when that snare finally breaks and a person stands on something solid, not on the shaky ground of whether people clap for them or not. I want you to see these not just as old stories, but as previews of your own future in Christ.

Abraham Lincoln

When you think back to the Civil War, it's easy to imagine Abraham Lincoln as this beloved, respected figure. But that's not how people saw him at the time. Newspapers tore him apart. They called him awkward, crude, unfit for office. Political cartoons mocked his appearance. Opponents called him "the ape." Even his own allies doubted him half the time.

But in the middle of all that noise, he just kept going. He did what he thought was right. He held the Union together. He showed mercy to the South when everyone else wanted revenge. He took hit after hit and didn't crumble. His strength didn't come from people cheering him on. It came from knowing what mattered.

Confidence isn't about nobody criticizing you. It's about being able to stand when everyone's pulling you in different directions. Lincoln's steadiness wasn't about being popular. It was about being anchored to something deeper.

Peter

Peter's story is wild because it shows that you can totally change. Remember when he was in that courtyard? A servant girl asked if he knew Jesus, and Peter folded. Three times. That's how powerful the fear of man is. It can shut down the boldest person in front of the smallest audience.

But then look at the same guy after Jesus restored him and the Spirit filled him. He's standing in front of the Sanhedrin, the most powerful religious council in Jerusalem. These men could throw him in prison. They could have him killed. And Peter looks them in the eye and says, "We have to obey God, not you" (see Acts 5:29).

What changed? Not his personality. What changed was where his confidence came from. It was rooted in the fact that Jesus rose from the dead and the Spirit was in Peter. The same mouth that once cursed and lied to save his own skin was now boldly preaching salvation to the same leaders who killed Jesus. That's the kind of transformation God can do in any of us. From scared to courageous. From silent to speaking truth.

Daniel

Daniel's whole life was basically a master class in confidence. When he was young and exiled in Babylon, he decided he wouldn't eat the king's rich food. Later, when they passed a law saying you couldn't pray to anyone but the king, Daniel could have compromised. He could have prayed quietly in his head. He could have waited for the law to expire.

But here's what Scripture says: "When Daniel knew that the document had been signed, he went to his house where he had windows in his upper chamber open toward Jerusalem. He got down on his knees three times a day and prayed and gave thanks before his God, as he had done previously" (Daniel 6:10).

That's confidence. Not showing off. Not being arrogant. Just refusing to let some decree silence his devotion to God. His courage got him thrown into a lions' den, but it also brought glory to God in front of an entire empire.

Christ Himself

And then there's Jesus. He understood people better than anyone. Scripture says, "But Jesus on his part did not entrust himself to them, because he knew all people and needed no one to bear witness about man, for he himself knew what was in man" (John 2:24–25). He saw right through praise and flattery. He knew the same crowd shouting "Hosanna!" one day could be yelling "Crucify Him!" the next. His confidence never came from whether people admired Him, because He knew how fickle and self-serving we all are.

Even His enemies saw this. When the Pharisees tried to trap Him with that question about paying taxes, they started by saying, "Teacher, we know that you are true and teach the way of God truthfully, and you do not care about anyone's opinion, for you are not swayed by appearances" (Matthew 22:16). In the original Greek, that last phrase literally means "you don't look at faces."[7] They were basically admitting that Jesus couldn't be manipulated. He didn't scan the room to figure out how bold He should be. He didn't change His message based on who was listening.

And here's the thing: That one line tells us something huge about how we're wired. We were made to "look at faces." Our brains do it automatically. Scientists even found a specific part of the brain called the fusiform face area that lights up when we see a face. In less than a second, we're reading emotion, status, familiarity, threat. God designed us this way so we can connect and stay safe in community. But it also makes us vulnerable. Because we're built to read faces, we often end up living for them. A frown can make us spiral. A nod can make us feel validated. The look in someone's eyes can completely shape how we see ourselves.

Jesus broke that pattern. He didn't "look at faces," because He was looking at His Father's face instead. His reference point wasn't the crowd. It was communion. Where everyone else drew confidence from human approval, He drew His from the Father's love.

So where did His confidence come from? From His Father's voice. At His baptism, the sky opened up and God said, "This is my beloved Son, with whom I am well pleased" (Matthew 3:17). That verdict carried Jesus through every rejection, every misunderstanding, every trial. He could take the scorn of people, because He was completely secure in His Father's delight. His confidence was unshakable because it was rooted in something eternal.

And that's the invitation for us. The same voice that spoke over Jesus speaks over every child of God: "You are my beloved." Until that truth gets louder than the crowd, we're always going to be tempted to live by what we see in people's faces instead of what we hear from heaven. (We'll come back to this later.)

The Doctor's Office

I was sitting in a doctor's office not long ago, just watching everything unfold. It was one of those busy practices where the doctor was doing everything. Secretary work, nurse work, doctor work. He was moving fast, getting people in and out, and I was just sitting there, watching him go.

Then something happened that completely changed how I think about confidence. He was helping this elderly woman out the door, being so careful and gentle with her. As he handed her off to his staff, I heard him say, "Be very careful with her. We don't want to rip her skin."

At first, I had this morbid curiosity. I wondered, *What's wrong with this woman, that her skin could just tear like tissue paper?* But then the Holy Spirit spoke to me about this doctor knowing who he was. He was a healer. He was confident in that. And because of that, her fragility didn't offend him. Her thin skin didn't frustrate him. It actually changed how he treated her. He saw her condition not as an inconvenience, but as a chance to show skill and compassion.

Because he knew who he was, he could handle her weakness with peace. He wasn't irritated that her skin was thin. He was confident that he was the doctor.

That's what healed confidence looks like. When you know who you are in Christ, you're not rattled by other people's fragility or their opinions. You're not frustrated by their weaknesses. You're steady. You're kind. You're free to live out your calling. Their thin skin doesn't threaten yours.

What God Is Doing in You

Picture with me what God is doing in you:

Imagine walking into a meeting and just saying what's true with kindness, without playing out every possible reaction in your head first.

Imagine standing with your friends and saying what you actually believe, even if nobody agrees.

Imagine praying with a co-worker who is in crisis, without feeling embarrassed.

Imagine leading your family with calm conviction instead of anxiously trying to please everyone.

Imagine looking in the mirror and just knowing your worth isn't on trial in somebody else's courtroom.

This isn't some fantasy. This is where Christ is taking you. Courage, peace, confidence. These aren't just for presidents, prophets, apostles, or doctors. They're what happens when a heart gets set free from needing everyone's approval and gets rooted instead in God's love.

In the next chapter, we've got one more chamber to look at: the chamber of memory. And then I'm going to show you how Christ heals your whole heart. How the Holy Spirit moves into every chamber and redeems every hurt, every fear, every cry for justice.

5

memory

the past that won't let go

Have you ever smelled Dial liquid soap?

John (not his real name) was in the Air Force. Some handle basic training better than others. John barely made it. During what he describes as six weeks of hell, every detail of his locker had to be spotless. Bar soap left residue that would have gotten him yelled at, so he switched to the liquid kind. He got used to the scent, clean and sharp and metallic, and never thought much about it again.

Years later, long after he had left the military, John found himself in a hospital waiting room. Someone walked by wearing that same scent of Dial soap, and before he could understand what was happening, his pulse spiked. His hands began to shake. His body went rigid. In an instant he was back in the barracks, under the shouting of instructors, feeling the pressure to perform and the fear of being recycled (the term used for sending airmen back a week or two in the training). To John, the idea that he could have to spend another minute in the place was the worst thing he could imagine.

The smell had pulled him through time.

That's how memory works. It is never fully buried. It hides until the right sound, taste, or smell opens the door again and you enter the chamber of memory. One small trigger, and suddenly the past is not past anymore. It breathes through your body. It speaks through your emotions. Have you ever had that happen? Sometimes even a certain kind of weather can do it. Usually it's a curiosity, but occasionally it can cause a full-blown meltdown.

I know of a man who had been unfaithful to his wife before they both came to Christ. After Jesus saved him, he confessed everything to her, and together they began to rebuild their marriage. They went through years of counseling. Over time, their marriage became something beautiful, full of grace, laughter, and purpose in building a ministry together. They raised children who loved God and loved them. The past was in the past, forgiven, redeemed, and seemingly forgotten.

Then one night years after the fact, they watched a movie about a man who had an affair. As the credits rolled, his wife was silent. In an instant, all the old pain returned as if it had happened yesterday. For weeks she spiraled into grief and anger, reliving a betrayal she had already forgiven. The husband could only pray and wonder if their marriage would survive.

It did. But that moment reminded them both that memory has a life of its own. What we think is finished often waits beneath the surface for a cue to reappear.

The Body Keeps the Score

A psychiatrist named Bessel van der Kolk wrote a book called *The Body Keeps the Score*. In its pages, he explains something really important: Trauma doesn't just live in your mind. It gets into your nervous system, your muscles, even your immune system. Long after you've told yourself, "I'm over it," your body is still holding on to the trauma, just waiting for something to remind it.

Like a lot of things, Scripture said this long before science gave it a name. David wrote in Psalm 32:3–4, "When I kept silent, my bones wasted away through my groaning all day long. For day and night your hand was heavy upon me; my strength was dried up as by the heat of summer." Memory, when it's not healed, gets into your body.

The chamber of memory is where everything still echoes. It holds the good stuff—laughter, joy, gratitude. But it also holds trauma, offense, broken promises. Some of my own memories make me grateful. Others still make my chest tighten. What we try to bury has a way of speaking again through our emotions and reactions. The past never really stays buried. It bleeds into today. It shapes how we see God, how we treat people.

Courage for the Past

I used to imagine Joshua staring at the walls of Jericho when God told him to be strong and courageous. Surely God was encouraging him, because He knew Joshua would need all the courage he could muster for the battles ahead. But lately, I think courage was needed not only for facing the future but for facing the wilderness behind him. Joshua carried forty years of loss and failure. Think about it: Almost every adult Joshua had left Egypt with was dead. Every grave in the desert was a reminder of what could have been.

The Hebrew word translated "be strong" in Joshua 1:9 is *chazaq*, which means to seize or to fasten oneself to something.[1] God was not telling Joshua to summon courage from within. He was telling him to fasten himself to the memory of His faithfulness.

That command still echoes today. We need courage not just to face what lies ahead, but to face what lives behind our smiles. I have learned that faith does not mean ignoring pain. God never asked me to forget the wilderness. He asked me to remember it truthfully. Joshua 4:1–7 says,

> When all the nation had finished passing over the Jordan, the Lord said to Joshua, "Take twelve men from the people, from each tribe a man, and command them, saying, 'Take twelve stones from here out of the midst of the Jordan, from the very place where the priests' feet stood firmly, and bring them over with you and lay them down in the place where you lodge tonight.'" Then Joshua called the twelve men from the people of Israel, whom he had appointed, a man from each tribe. And Joshua said to them, "Pass on before the ark of the Lord your God into the midst of the Jordan, and take up each of you a stone upon his shoulder, according to the number of the tribes of the people of Israel, that this may be a sign among you. When your children ask in time to come, 'What do those stones mean to you?' then you shall tell them that the waters of the Jordan were cut off before the ark of the covenant of the Lord. When it passed over the Jordan, the waters of the Jordan were cut off. So these stones shall be to the people of Israel a memorial forever."

The stones the twelve men of Israel carried from the Jordan were not trophies. They were testimonies. They told the truth about deliverance through pain. Memory can be a prison or a passageway, depending on whether it is faced in truth.

The Bee Sting of Unresolved Memory

There was a time I told myself I had forgiven someone who betrayed me. I even preached sermons about forgiveness, quoting all the right verses, smiling while I said them. I wanted it to be true. I really wanted to believe I was free. But every time the person's name came up, something in me clenched. My jaw tightened. My chest got hot. I could feel the reaction before I could even think about it. It was as if the wound had never closed.

That's the thing about wounds. They might scab over, but if they're not cleaned out, infection spreads quietly underneath. You can look healed and still be sick.

A bee leaves its stinger behind. The wound looks small, but the venom keeps spreading until you pull the stinger out. That's how unresolved memory works. Forgiveness pulls out the stinger, but truth drains the poison. I had said the words "I forgive," but the venom of resentment was still running through me. I was living with spiritual toxins, smiling while I poisoned myself.

At first, I blamed the other person for every flash of anger that came up. But after a while, I started noticing something. The problem wasn't just that person. It was the memory. The betrayal was over, but the echo wasn't. Every time something even slightly resembled that old pain, my body reacted as though it were happening all over again. A certain tone of voice. A decision made without asking me. A friend who seemed to pull away. Suddenly I was back in the same emotional storm, replaying the same arguments in my head.

That's how you know the venom is still there. The moment is gone, but the reaction is still alive.

Jesus said in Mark 11:25, "Whenever you stand praying, forgive, if you have anything against anyone." Forgiveness isn't about emotion. It's about obedience. But obedience feels totally unnatural when the wound is still fresh. You want justice, not surrender. You want closure, not humility. But Jesus connects forgiveness directly to prayer. Why? Because unforgiveness blocks the flow of God's presence in your life.

When you refuse to release someone, the memory keeps releasing its venom into you. It leaks out in sarcasm, control, defensiveness, withdrawal. It seeps into your relationships. You start seeing people not as they are, but as your pain tells you they are.

That's why Jesus used such strong language when He taught on forgiveness. In Matthew 18, He tells the story of a servant who was forgiven a huge debt, but refused to forgive someone who owed him pocket change. When the master found out, he "handed him over to the jailers to be tortured, until he should pay back all he owed" (verse 34 NIV). It's a hard story. But it's a perfect picture of what happens in the chamber of memory.

Unforgiveness is self-imposed captivity. You hand yourself over to the tormentors of anxiety, fear, and bitterness. You live chained to the memory of what someone else did. And here's the thing: The punishment isn't for the person who hurt you. It's for you, the one refusing to let go.

A lot of believers live this way. Reacting to old wounds instead of responding to the Spirit. They think they're angry with the people in front of them, but they're really angry with ghosts from the past. The smallest slight can open a floodgate because it touches a place that never healed. And most of us don't even realize how much we're still bleeding until we see the stain.

That's the power of unresolved memory. It keeps you living yesterday's pain in today's relationships. You think you're reacting to what's happening now, but you're actually just trying to protect yourself from what happened back then.

I wish I could say I learned this lesson fast, but the truth is, I carried that stinger for years. I prayed for peace but felt unrest. I asked for joy but felt numb. Until the poison is drawn out, even your prayers feel heavy. The words come out, but they don't lift. Something in you still remembers. And it won't let you rest.

God of Time and Redeemed Memories

There was a day God asked me to go back to an actual physical place where part of me had broken.

I told Him I was healed. I told Him it wasn't necessary. I even told myself I was being dramatic for feeling nervous about it. But obedience has a way of exposing what denial hides, and I could feel something deeper stirring inside me. Something unhealed.

When I got to the location, the air itself felt heavy. It was as if the room still remembered what had happened. Every detail came flooding back. The sound of footsteps. The tone of a voice. That sharp scent that used to hang in the air. My body tensed before my mind could even catch up. Memory doesn't knock politely. It just walks right in.

Standing there, I felt every old emotion surge up again. Anger. Shame. Disappointment. I whispered out loud, *God, where were You when this happened?*

And in the quiet, I felt His answer: *I was there*.

I didn't know what to do with that. It sounded impossible. How could He have been there and let it happen? If He was really there, why did it still hurt so much? His words didn't erase anything. They opened something. They invited me to wonder if maybe His presence hadn't been absent after all. Just unseen.

That thought unsettled me even more. It's easier to believe that God abandoned you than to face the mystery that He was present and still allowed the wound. That tension, His sovereignty and my pain, became a question I couldn't stop asking.

Ecclesiastes 3:15 (NIV) says, "Whatever is has already been, and what will be has been before; and God will call the past to account." That verse doesn't mean God replays our mistakes over and over. It means He revisits our story. He calls every moment, past, present, and future, back under His authority. He doesn't skip over our history. He reclaims it.

Maybe one day I'll see clearly how He was working in those moments I wanted to erase. Maybe one day I'll understand what He was doing while I was breaking. For now, I'm learning to live with the question. Trusting that His presence is larger than my understanding.

I believe the day will come when He shows me what He was doing. Not to justify what happened, but to redeem the memory. That's part of what this book is about. But I'm not there yet. Right now, I'm still standing in that quiet place between pain and promise. Learning to let the question linger, without losing faith.

The Note in the Drawer

Not every memory is painful. Some carry promise.

When John smells Dial soap, he still remembers the pressure and fear of basic training. But he also remembers the friendships that got forged in that fire. Those young men shared everything—terror, exhaustion, and the pride of surviving together. They laughed in the face of the same storms and carried each other through sleepless nights. That scent doesn't only pull John back into stress. It brings back the brotherhood that formed right in the middle of it.

For me, a good memory came when I found something. When I was a teenager, I had scribbled some words on a piece of notebook paper: "Senior Pastor Mike Signorelli." I folded it up and tucked it into a drawer, then forgot about it for years. One day I found it again, after God had made it true. That small scrap of paper reminded me that memory can hold prophecy. God had planted a seed of calling in me before I ever knew what it meant.

Joseph's dreams must have been the same way. In the darkness of that prison, he could look back on those dreams and remember that God had spoken. His memories became evidence that his story still had purpose.

In the same way, some of our memories are promises just waiting to be fulfilled. But in this stage of the journey, I'm still learning that those promises often live right alongside the pain.

The Weight of Inheritance

Not all memory is personal. Some of it is inherited. We carry stories we never lived and wounds we never received directly. Every family hands down more than eye color or last names. We inherit ways of coping, ways of speaking, and ways of hiding.

In my family, we were taught to be strong. We didn't talk much about pain. We worked hard. We kept going. We believed that endurance was the same thing as faith. I remember hearing "it'll be fine" a lot more than I ever heard "how do you feel?"

We didn't mean to pass that silence along. It was survival. My parents learned it from their parents, and their parents from the ones before them. It was the language of people who had seen disappointment and learned not to expect too much. For a long time, I thought that was maturity. Getting over things quickly. Not crying. Moving on. But I see now it was fear wearing the mask of toughness.

Those patterns live in us longer than we realize. They shape the way we love and the way we worship. They teach us to hide behind competence or humor or ministry. They whisper that strength means silence.

Earlier in this chapter, I mentioned *The Body Keeps the Score*. In that book, Dr. Bessel van der Kolk showed that trauma doesn't disappear with time. It takes up residence in the body. It lodges itself in the brain's alarm systems and muscle memory so deeply that even decades later, the body still braces for a threat that no longer exists. But what Van der Kolk discovered about individuals, neuroscientist Rachel Yehuda found to be true across generations.

Yehuda has spent more than three decades studying Holocaust survivors and their descendants. She found that trauma leaves chemical marks on DNA that can alter how genes are expressed. These aren't changes in the genetic code itself, but in how that code is read and activated. She calls this process *epigenetic inheritance*. In simple terms, the body learns from experience and passes that learning on.

Children and grandchildren of survivors were born with lower levels of cortisol, the hormone that helps regulate stress. Their bodies, before they ever faced danger, were already prepared to live on high alert. It's as if their physiology had been trained to expect threat, to hold its breath waiting for the next blow. They weren't traumatized by direct experience, but by biology's memory of trauma.

When I first read that, I had to stop and sit with it. The idea that suffering can echo through cells, that fear can become part of the body's architecture, was both heartbreaking and strangely affirming. It told me something Scripture had been saying all along: that the wounds of one generation ripple into the next until someone lets God heal them.

Yehuda's research has since been replicated with children of combat veterans, victims of abuse, and even communities living under long-term oppression. What she found is that the body's stress response is like an inheritance. A genetic sermon preached without words, teaching the next generation how to survive. The problem is that survival mode doesn't know how to rest. It protects, but it doesn't trust.

When in Exodus 20:5 the Lord said that the sins of the fathers would be visited upon the children to the third and fourth generation, He wasn't describing punishment as much as pattern. Pain that isn't confessed becomes transmitted. Yehuda's findings show what that looks like on a molecular level. What the Bible calls a generational curse, science now calls gene expression. Both are describing the same reality: that we're not as separate from our ancestors as we think.

But Yehuda also offers hope. She found that healing, too, can be inherited. When survivors found safety, love, and community, the stress responses in their children began to change. The same mechanism that preserved pain could also transmit peace. The human body, like the human soul, is designed for redemption.

When I read Yehuda's work, I think of my own family. The constant striving. The anxiety under the surface. The inability to rest. It wasn't just personality. It was inheritance. Our bodies had learned to brace for loss. But if stress could be handed down, maybe peace could be too.

Yehuda is joined by voices across the spectrum of psychology and theology. Likewise, physician Gabor Maté says that pain not transformed will always be transmitted. He has spent years working with families who carry suffering that's older than they are. When people grow up in homes where pain is suppressed, he says, the body itself becomes the storyteller. Grief that's never spoken often reappears as anxiety, addiction, or chronic illness. In his words, "Trauma is not what happens to you; it's what happens inside you as a result of what happens to you."[2] And if that inner wound never finds healing, it becomes the unspoken inheritance of a family line.

Children absorb the emotional atmosphere of a home, though they may never have the words or understanding to describe it. Silence, fear, shame, and unresolved pain become the air they breathe. These shape their understanding of everyone involved—themselves, others, even God. But the Holy Spirit is not intimidated by any climate. He has the power to move through generations and bring healing, even where pain has been passed down for centuries. He restores what's been distorted.

Neil Anderson describes strongholds as entrenched patterns of thinking that keep people from experiencing freedom. The tragedy is forgetting that Christ purchased this for them. Anderson reminds believers, "Don't wait to forgive until you feel like forgiving; you will never get there. Feelings take time to heal after the choice to forgive is made."[3] It's true that freedom begins with forgiveness, but it is learning to walk in that freedom that is a continuing work and takes time.

After I read these voices, I began to see my own story differently. I understood why silence felt safer than honesty. Why I pushed through exhaustion instead of asking for help. Why I avoided conflict by pretending peace. Those weren't just habits. They were inherited reflexes.

The Israelites carried Egypt inside them long after they crossed the sea. They remembered slavery more vividly than freedom.

Even when manna fell from heaven, they longed for the food of their captivity. I understand that now. It's easier to crave familiar pain than to trust unfamiliar grace.

Sometimes I wonder what Egypt I still carry. What memories and messages still whisper in me from generations ago. Some of them are good: perseverance, resourcefulness, faithfulness to family. Others are heavier: the need to prove myself, the instinct to fix rather than feel, the fear of being weak.

Every generation hands down a way of interpreting pain. Some call it a heritage. God calls it a pattern. Until those patterns are named, they can't be broken.

I believe there is freedom beyond what I inherited. I believe God rewrites family stories. But I'm still learning how to name the weight before I can lay it down.

The Courage to Remember

For a long time, I believed that avoiding pain was the same as overcoming it. Ministry kept me busy. Success covered a lot of wounds.

But unhealed memory is like mold under paint. You can hide it, but it grows in the dark. Eventually, it makes itself known on the surface. But all along, it has been causing problems in secret.

God never asked me to forget. He invited me to remember differently. But I'm not ready to talk about what that looks like yet. That's for later. For now, the lesson is simpler and harder at the same time: Avoided memories control us more than remembered ones.

What you refuse to face continues to define you. The Holy Spirit isn't afraid of your past. But until you stop running from it, He will wait at the door. Healing doesn't begin with closure. It begins with courage.

So before we move forward, I want you to look inward.

A Memory Inventory

Before you turn the page, pause. Take a breath. Let the Holy Spirit bring to mind things you may not have visited in years.

You might be surprised by what rises to the surface when you give yourself permission to remember. Ask yourself:

Do I ever feel an instant rush of anger, shame, or defensiveness before I can even explain why?

Are there names I still avoid saying out loud because of what they represent?

Is there a song, a place, or a smell that makes me uneasy, even though nothing is wrong in the present moment?

Have I ever found myself reliving an argument long after it ended, again and again replaying what I should have said?

Do certain family gatherings fill me with dread or exhaustion even before I get there?

When someone praises me, do I instinctively downplay it or change the subject?

Do I struggle to trust compliments, believing deep down that people are just being polite?

Have I ever succeeded at something and felt sad instead of happy, like joy was off-limits to me?

Do I find it hard to rest, afraid that slowing down will let old thoughts catch up?

Are there seasons of my life that feel like sealed rooms—college, childhood, an old relationship—that I rarely let myself visit?

Do I sometimes feel guilt for things that weren't my fault but became my responsibility anyway?

Are there moments when I feel small in the presence of authority, even if no one is mistreating me?

Have I noticed that certain tones of voice make me react strongly before I even process what was said?

Do I still feel the need to defend myself for something that happened a long time ago?

When someone betrays my trust, do I react to the person, or to the memory of everyone who ever has betrayed me?

Do I carry stories from my family—losses, failures, or secrets—that shape how I see myself even now?

Do I ever look at old photos and feel an ache I can't explain, as if part of me is still there?

Have I ever noticed how a smell, a song, or a movie scene can bring tears to my eyes before my mind catches up to why?

Do I sometimes feel as if I'm living two lives: the one I show to others, and the one that replays in my mind when things go quiet?

The First Step Toward Redemption

If you found yourself nodding yes to more than one of these questions, that's not failure. It's evidence that the chamber of memory is still alive in you. It means there are places in your story that still echo. And that God still wants to visit.

So don't rush past this. The fact that you can feel these things isn't proof that you are broken beyond repair. It's proof that your heart still remembers. And that remembering is the first step toward redemption.

The answers are coming. Healing is coming. But first, the truth has to be named.

You can't heal what you won't face. And you can't face what you refuse to remember.

part two

the healing process

6

going deep into the heart

Have you ever heard of the Hero's Journey?

It's the backbone of almost every great story ever told. *The Odyssey*. *The Matrix*. Moses. Modern movies. The pattern is always the same: Someone gets called to adventure, crosses a threshold, faces a series of trials, descends into darkness, and then, if grace has its way, rises again.

But somewhere in the middle of that journey, there's always a descent. The hero has to go down before he can come back up. He gets stripped of everything. Control. Weapons. Certainty. It's the moment when the story gets quiet and heavy. The cave. The tomb. The place where every illusion finally dies.

And that cave looks different for everyone.

For Joseph, it was the pit his brothers threw him into. A literal hole in the ground that smelled like dust and betrayal. One moment he's the favored son, wrapped in that colorful coat. The next, he's stripped down to nothing, staring up at a piece of sky he can't reach anymore. The dreamer who had seen visions of greatness was left wondering if maybe he had only been dreaming of dirt. His descent started the moment the people closest to him decided he wasn't worth keeping.

For Jonah, the cave was the belly of a fish. The walls pulsed around him like a living coffin. Darkness pressed in from every side. Salt and acid burned his throat. There were no crowds down there. No pulpit. No platform. Just the sound of his own heartbeat echoing off the ribs of his consequences. Jonah had run from God, and now there was nowhere left to run. The sea had swallowed him whole, and even his prayers came out muffled and half-believed. Can you relate?

For Daniel, the descent didn't come through rebellion. It came through obedience. He hadn't run from God. He had refused to bow to anyone else. And his reward? A den full of lions. He could feel their breath in the dark. Hot. Heavy. The scrape of claws on stone. Courage in that place didn't roar. It whispered. It whispered trust in a God who shuts the mouths of predators, but sometimes waits until morning to rescue us.

But for Jesus, the cave wasn't the tomb. It was the cross. The place where He hung between heaven and earth. Exposed. Rejected. Stripped of every protection. The cross was His descent into total surrender. Even though He was perfect and didn't need to change, Scripture says that "he learned obedience through what he suffered" (Hebrews 5:8). The same passage tells us He was "made perfect" (verse 9), which means complete and fully prepared, through suffering.

On the cross, Jesus experienced the full weight of our darkness. The silence of the Father. The mockery of the crowd. The crushing loneliness of being misunderstood, abandoned, and despised. The One who had healed others now bled without help. The One who had raised the dead now faced His own death. Yet for "the joy that was set before him," He endured it all (Hebrews 12:2). If even Jesus, though sinless, was perfected and prepared through His cave moment, why wouldn't we also be prepared that way?

The cross wasn't just an act of redemption. It was an act of revelation. And it showed us what love looks like when it refuses to defend itself. Not only did Jesus secure His own joy through His cave moment, but He secured ours as well. And also our healing.

The pit. The fish. The den. The cross. Each is a doorway disguised as disaster. Each brings the hero face-to-face with what must die before life can truly begin.

That same pattern shows up in our stories too. The cave might be a diagnosis. A divorce. A betrayal. A long silence from heaven when you thought an answer was coming. The shape changes, but the purpose doesn't. God still leads His people into darkness—not to destroy them, but to reveal what light alone cannot show.

Exposing the Monster Within

Do you know the movie series *Star Wars*? I think of Luke Skywalker on the planet Dagobah. It's one of the most haunting scenes in cinema. His training with Yoda has been going well enough. Lifting rocks. Balancing on one hand. Learning to focus. But then Yoda points toward a shadowy opening beneath the twisted roots of an ancient tree. The air seems to hum with danger.

"What's in there?" Luke asks.

"Only what you take with you," Yoda says.[1]

Luke tightens his belt, grabs his lightsaber, and steps into the dark. The air is thick and wet. Every sound is magnified. The drip of water. The rustle of unseen creatures. The quick rhythm of his own breath inside his helmet. Then, out of the mist, Darth Vader appears!

The red blade flashes. The cave fills with the violent dance of light and shadow. Luke strikes fast, driven by fear more than faith, and the enemy falls. The black mask rolls across the ground, hissing open as it lands.

But then, something utterly surprising happens.

Inside the helmet, it's not Vader's face. It's Luke's own.

He stares in shock. George Lucas wants the meaning to hit harder than any blow from a lightsaber.

The darkness Luke fears lives inside him.

That's what every cave reveals.

You go in thinking you're going to fight the monster outside you, only to find the reflection of the monster within. You think you're battling the people who hurt you, but in the half-light you see the same pride, the same need for control, the same hunger for justification staring back.

That's what happened to me. When I prayed for God to heal my heart, I thought I was asking Him to remove the pain. What He was really doing was inviting me to die to the pride, the self-righteousness, and the defenses I had built to keep pain out—and kept love out with it.

You can't heal what you still protect. And I was still protecting my heart.

The descent isn't about destruction. It's about exposure. It's where God shows you what cannot come with you into resurrection. It's where you stop blaming everyone else and whisper, *Maybe the real fight is in me.*

Every resurrection begins with a death, and every death begins in a cave.

Or a fish, a pit, or a lions' den. Or, more accurately, a cross. It's the cross that we pick up and carry as we lose our life to find it (see Matthew 16:24–25).

If you're reading this and feel that quiet weight, the exhaustion, the emptiness, the realization that you cannot fix yourself, you're not failing. You're being invited.

This is the moment before new life. The silence before the stone rolls away. The deepest part of the journey, where you discover that healing doesn't come from climbing higher, but from surrendering lower.

You're not alone there. God does His best work in caves.

The Hardest Confrontation

It is one thing to face what others have done to you. It is another thing entirely to face what you have done to others.

Up to this point, the story of offense has been about survival.

You have looked at the betrayals, the disappointments, the injustices that shaped your heart. You have seen the people who wounded you and maybe even forgiven them in theory. But something happens when you linger there too long. You start to realize that pain rarely stays put. It leaks. And often, without meaning to, you have carried your own fire into someone else's story.

I remember when that truth started to dawn on me. It was not a single dramatic revelation, but more like the slow rising of light I did not ask for.

The Holy Spirit has this way of showing you yourself in layers. At first, I could only see the familiar film reel of what others had done wrong. Then, like a photograph developing in a darkroom, another image appeared underneath. There I was, doing the same things I despised. Speaking the sharp words. Shutting down when someone needed comfort. Telling myself I was defending my heart when I was really hardening it. I had been so busy trying to be right that I forgot how to be kind.

That was the moment I understood that offense is contagious. The wound you refuse to face in yourself, you end up inflicting on someone else.

It is strange how easily we spot pride in others and how hard it is to see it in our own reflection. I used to think of pride as arrogance, loud and obvious, but mine was quieter than that. It wore a prayer shawl. It quoted Scripture. It led worship. It said things like "I am just trying to help," when the truth was that I wanted control. Pride does not always boast. Sometimes it hides behind humility that is not real.

Jeremiah once wrote, "The heart is deceitful above all things, and desperately sick; who can understand it?" (Jeremiah 17:9). I had read that verse many times, but it landed differently when I finally realized it was not about other people. It was about me. The heart that needed healing was my own.

God's first step toward healing isn't comfort. It's exposure. He won't clean what you insist on covering. And when He starts lifting those covers, it can feel brutal at first. But it's mercy, even when it hurts.

David once prayed, "Search me, O God, and know my heart! Try me and know my thoughts!" (Psalm 139:23). I used to think that was just a poetic way to sound spiritual. Then one day, God actually answered it in me. When He does that, you learn really fast that He takes prayers like that literally. He starts pointing out patterns that used to feel like safety but are really just self-protection. He shows you habits that make you look strong but quietly keep you isolated. He shines a light on bitterness you've been calling discernment, and control you've been calling care.

You start to notice that your anger isn't always righteous. Sometimes it's just fear with a sword in its hand.

Your silence isn't always peace. Sometimes it's punishment.

Your independence isn't always faith. Sometimes it's just the fear of being disappointed again.

I remember sitting in my car one night after a disagreement that should've been simple. I told myself the other person was wrong. And maybe that was true. But underneath all my arguments, I heard a quieter voice asking, *Why does being right matter so much to you?*

I didn't have an answer.

That's the hardest confrontation. When you stop replaying what other people did and start asking what's happening inside you. When you stop asking, *Why did they?* and start asking, *Why do I?*

I started to see that offense doesn't just build walls. It builds identities. I had made being misunderstood part of who I was. It felt safe. It let me stay distant while pretending to be discerning. I could play the victim and still feel superior. I told myself, *They just don't get me*, when what I really meant was *I don't want to risk being known.*

And that's the subtle cruelty of pride. It often looks like maturity. You call it calmness, but it's really numbness. You call it wisdom, but it's cynicism dressed in faith's clothes.

The more I looked, the more I saw my own reflection in the faces of the people who had hurt me. It wasn't shame I felt, though it could have been.

It was weariness.

I was tired of defending myself. I was tired of managing my image. I was tired of pretending I was healed, while still bleeding on people who hadn't cut me.

God's mercy, I've learned, isn't sentimental. It's surgical. Before He resurrects a heart, He opens it. Before He comforts, He confronts. Before He fills, He empties.

That might sound harsh, but it's strangely freeing. When everything false finally falls apart, you can breathe again. You stop pretending to be better than you are. You stop performing strength and finally let God be the one who is good.

So if you find yourself in that mirror right now, seeing both the wound and the wounder, don't look away. This isn't condemnation. It's invitation.

Yes, the cave feels darker now. But that means you're closer to the center. The hardest confrontation is never with another person. It's with your own heart.

And even here, grace is waiting.

The Root of Pride

If I follow offense deep enough, it always leads me to the same place. Pride. Not the loud kind that brags or demands attention, but the quiet kind that hides behind hurt. The kind that calls itself strength.

It rarely looks like pride at first. It looks like maturity. Or wisdom. Or healthy boundaries. It tells me I am guarding my peace, but in reality, I am guarding my pain.

I used to think pride started with arrogance, with people who talked too much about themselves. But I have learned it usually begins with blindness. Pride is sneaky that way. You can't see it in yourself because it is always looking outward. It's like a smudge on a mirror that only shows up when someone else stands in front of it.

I see it in the story of Lucifer. He looked at his own beauty until he began to worship it. He said, "I will ascend. . . . I will make myself like the Most High" (Isaiah 14:14). That one decision cracked heaven open. Pride turned an angel into an enemy of God. And it still does the same thing to people like me. It turns the heart into a small kingdom where I'm the only one on the throne.

My own pride rarely looks that dramatic. It slips in through self-reliance. It teaches me to depend on myself when I feel unseen by others, to protect myself when love feels risky. It may sound like confidence, but it's really fear dressed up as strength.

For a long time, I quoted Proverbs 4:23 as my excuse for retreat: "Guard your heart, for everything you do flows from it" (NIV). I told myself I was being wise. But guarding my heart slowly became fortifying it. The verse doesn't say to build walls around your heart; it says to watch over it. To guard means to stay attentive, to remain open, to keep it soft before God. I wasn't guarding my heart for Him. I was guarding it from people. There's a difference, and that difference matters.

Protection keeps you alive. Isolation keeps you alone.

I used to think pride was about thinking too highly of myself. That's easy to spot.

The harder kind is when I can't stop thinking about myself at all. Even my insecurity can be a form of pride because I'm still the center of every thought. It's exhausting, living like that. Every conversation gets filtered through how it makes me look. Every silence feels like rejection.

Even my prayers used to sound like pride sometimes. *God, help me. Change me. Fix me.* Every line started and ended with *me*. It was as if I was trying to manage my own sanctification.

I wanted transformation, but not surrender.

Healing, but not exposure.

Resurrection, but not crucifixion.

The truth is, pride is a refusal to trust. It believes that God won't come through unless I control the terms. It sounds wise. It feels safe. But it suffocates the soul.

I've caught myself doing it more times than I can count. I want God to heal my heart, but I keep grabbing the knife from the Surgeon. I tell Him where to cut, how deep to go, and when to stop. But you can't perform your own surgery. You have to lie still and trust the hands that know what they're doing.

Scripture says of Jesus that He, "being in very nature God, did not consider equality with God something to be used to his own advantage; rather, he made himself nothing by taking the very nature of a servant" (Philippians 2:6–7 NIV). That passage undoes me. Pride clings. Humility opens its hand. Jesus descended before He ascended. His way down became our way home.

Pride builds the walls. Humility builds the bridge. Pride says, "I can handle this." Humility admits, "I can't, and that's where love begins."

Every time I hold on to offense, pride is somewhere beneath it. It might not look like superiority. It might look like fear. I don't want to forgive, because forgiveness feels like losing. I don't want to be wrong, because being right feels like survival. I don't want to let go, because control feels like peace.

But pride is counterfeit strength. It works for a while. You do get tougher. People even respect you for it. But something in you hardens. You stop feeling. You stop growing. Your world shrinks until it fits only you.

There's a point in every story where the hero realizes all his striving can't save him. The armor that once kept him safe is now keeping him from being touched. That's where pride has to die.

God doesn't humble us to humiliate us. He humbles us to free us. To help us breathe again. To remind us that we were never meant to carry our own redemption.

When I feel that unmasking—the ache, the discomfort, the loss of control—I try to remember it's not punishment. It might actually be mercy. God isn't taking something from me. He's removing what has been taking from me all along.

Pride built the walls. But grace is already knocking at the door.

The Shadow of Control

If pride is the root, control is what grows from it. I didn't see that for a long time. Control felt like wisdom to me. It felt like strength. It felt like doing what any responsible person should do when life starts slipping apart.

But looking back, I can see what it really was. Fear wearing a confident face.

I used to tell myself, *I'm just trying to be a good leader*, or *I'm only making sure this doesn't fall apart again*. Those sounded mature. Even noble. But underneath, I was afraid. Afraid of chaos. Of being blindsided. Of being hurt again. I thought letting go would make me weak or foolish. I didn't realize that my need to manage everything was actually a quiet confession of unbelief.

There's that verse "Be still, and know that I am God" (Psalm 46:10). I used to quote it as though I understood it. The truth is, I didn't know how to be still. Stillness felt like danger. My whole life had been built on movement. Fixing. Keeping everything together. I wanted to know that He is God, but I also wanted to make sure He did things my way.

Control, at least in my life, rarely announced itself as rebellion. It showed up as over-responsibility. I called it stewardship, as if I were doing God a favor by managing His outcomes. I planned. I organized. I delegated. Sometimes I prayed. But mostly I just tried to stay in charge of how everything turned out.

Even when I started asking God to heal my heart, I caught myself trying to control that too. I wanted Him to move, but on my schedule. I wanted transformation without discomfort. I wanted to trust Him as long as the process stayed predictable.

The truth is, I've spent a lot of my life trying to keep pain on a leash. I didn't want to feel helpless again, so I gripped everything tighter. Plans. People. Even my own emotions. Control became my version of safety. I thought I was protecting myself, but I was really just keeping myself stuck.

It might sound strange, but control is a kind of self-worship. It places faith in my own ability to prevent what I fear. It says, *As long as I stay vigilant, I'll be okay*. That belief might get you through a season or two, but it drains the soul over time. Preparation without surrender turns into self-preservation. And self-preservation eventually isolates you from both people and God.

The story of Peter walking on the water always gets to me. He steps out of the boat, full of courage, eyes locked on Jesus. But then the wind picks up. The waves get loud. And Peter's attention shifts from Jesus to the storm. That feels familiar. I want to walk by faith, but I keep noticing the wind. The bills. The opinions. The deadlines. The what-ifs. Before I know it, I'm sinking in the same water I was invited to walk on.

I don't think God punishes us for that instinct to control. I think He just lets us feel its limits. He lets the water rise high enough that we finally reach for His hand instead of our own plan.

Jesus once told Peter, "When you were younger you dressed yourself and went where you wanted; but when you are old . . . someone else will dress you and lead you where you do not want to go" (John 21:18 NIV). I used to think that was only about Peter's death. Now it sounds like the story of discipleship itself. When I was young in faith, I ran on self-reliance. I had my plans. My goals. My certainty. But as I've grown, I've learned that maturity looks a lot more like surrender than control. God leads me into places I wouldn't have chosen. And that's where I finally find freedom.

Control feels safe, but it's not. It's only familiar. It tells you that if you can manage enough variables, you can avoid pain. But the cave of control always ends the same way. In exhaustion.

I'm still learning this. Some days, I surrender everything. Other days, I take it all back before lunch. But even that awareness feels like progress. It means I'm noticing what I used to ignore.

I've started to believe that freedom comes less from figuring things out and more from letting go of what I was never meant to carry. The tighter I hold on, the smaller my world becomes.

Control was never my strength. It was my fear pretending to be faith. And fear can't coexist with perfect love.

So I open my hands again. Not perfectly. Not permanently. But enough for today.

Because the longer I live, the more I realize that the only thing harder than letting go is admitting that I was never really holding it in the first place.

The Unhealed Offender

There comes a point in the cave when you stop defending yourself and start remembering faces.

I still see them. Not the people who've hurt me, but the ones I've hurt. Some of them probably wouldn't even use that word. They might say we lost touch, or that life just moved on. But I know better. I can still feel the weight of moments when I shut down, pulled back, or spoke in a tone that landed harder than I intended.

For a long time, I told myself I didn't mean it. And maybe I didn't. But meaning well doesn't cancel the damage.

It's strange when it hits you—the realization that you can be both the healed victim in one story and the offender in another. You can pray for mercy and then, a few hours later, refuse to give it. You can sing about grace and still be stingy with it. You can tell people about forgiveness while quietly keeping score.

That's the part of the cave I didn't expect. The mirror doesn't just show your scars; it shows your shadow.

Paul captured it better than anyone in Romans 7:15: "I do the very thing I hate." I used to read that as theology. Now I read it as biography. I know what it feels like to want to love someone well but to keep finding the same old patterns waiting for me at the surface. Fear. Pride. Control. They show up before I realize I've opened the door.

Maybe you've seen that in yourself too. You tried to be gentle but came across cold. You meant to be honest but ended up being cruel. You wanted to protect someone and accidentally pushed the person away. It's a humbling moment when you realize your healing hasn't yet made you safe for others.

I used to think that my being forgiven by God meant people could automatically trust me again. It doesn't work like that. Forgiveness is free; trust is earned. To be honest, I hadn't learned how to earn it.

At some point, I asked God to show me where my unhealed places had spilled onto others. I expected a vague sense of conviction, something general. But God is not vague. He is personal. He started showing me faces.

One of them was a friend whose calls I stopped returning because the person's pain made me uncomfortable. Another was a family member I quietly resented while pretending everything was fine. There was a leader I criticized behind closed doors while convincing myself I was just "being truthful."

Each time, I tried to shrug it off: *That was years ago. They're fine now.* But the memories wouldn't leave. They were not accusations. They were invitations.

When the Holy Spirit reveals these things, it doesn't feel like shame. It's more like the sting of cleaning a wound. It hurts, but only because infection has to be exposed before it can heal.

If someone's face or name is coming to mind as you read this, don't brush it away. That might not be guilt. It might be grace. God doesn't show us these things to crush us. He shows them so we can finally stop pretending that our part doesn't matter.

The cave has a way of quieting everything that usually keeps us distracted. All the noise. All the busyness. All the ways we stay one step ahead of what we're feeling. In that silence, you can finally hear your excuses for what they really are. Small. Tired. Hollow. Like lines you've rehearsed so many times you forgot they weren't true. You start to realize the story you've been telling yourself isn't the whole story. There's another side to it, and you've left your fingerprints all over it.

I remember praying, *God, make me whole*, not realizing what I was actually asking for. I thought wholeness would feel peaceful. You know, like that long exhale after years of holding your breath. I pictured something calm and simple, where the pain would finally make sense and the past would stop echoing around in my head the way it does late at night when I can't sleep.

But wholeness, at least in my life, started with seeing the whole truth about myself. Not the version I show people at church or work. Not even the version I try to believe in my better moments, when I'm feeling pretty good about how I'm doing. But the one that stands completely bare before God. No spin. No filters. No "Yeah, but . . ."

That kind of truth doesn't shout at you. It doesn't accuse. It just sits there, patiently, waiting for you to stop talking long enough to actually hear it.

Sometimes after I pray, I feel this weight settle over me. Not heavy in a crushing way, but heavy as though something real just landed. I used to think it was guilt. Condemnation. God being disappointed in me again. But I think now it's actually honesty. It's the slow, heavy awareness that I've spent a lot of my life trying to look healed instead of actually being healed. Trying to perform peace instead of letting God actually create it in me. Trying to manage people's perceptions of me instead of letting God do the real work under the surface.

Wholeness isn't soft or sentimental. It's not a gentle process with candlelight and worship music in the background. It's more like being cracked open so the light can finally get in. It exposes the places where good intentions still hurt people. Where love mixed with fear still leaves wounds. Where self-protection starts to look an awful lot like pride dressed up in spiritual language.

There are moments when the truth hits me so clearly that I literally can't move. I just sit in the stillness and say, *Okay, Lord. This is me. All of me.* And that moment, as uncomfortable as it is, feels sacred.

Wholeness isn't only about being forgiven. It's about becoming the kind of person who stops passing pain along to other people. It's learning how to stay open when everything in you wants to shut down. It's finding the courage to tell the truth about what hurts, without using that truth as a weapon against anyone else.

That's the kind of healing I want now. Not the kind that makes me look spiritual, but the kind that makes me human again. I want to be someone who doesn't make other people pay for the pain I'm refusing to deal with.

But getting there feels like dying.

It feels like the death of self-protection. All those walls I built to keep myself safe. The death of denial. All those stories I told myself so I could stay blameless. The death of needing to be right, which might be the hardest thing to let go of.

When those things start falling apart, it doesn't feel holy at all. It feels like loss. You start wondering who you're even going to be without all that scaffolding holding you up. You feel exposed. Small. Unsure of where you stand anymore. But maybe that's what resurrection actually requires. An honest burial before any new life can grow.

Maybe this is how God rebuilds us.

We're all wounded people learning not to wound other people. All forgiven, still learning how to forgive. All offenders, desperately in need of the same mercy we keep asking for.

The cave isn't a courtroom. It's a place of surgery. God doesn't put you on trial here. He just tells you the truth. And truth, when it's spoken in love, cuts before it heals.

If you'll let Him, He'll hold the light steady long enough for you to see what you couldn't face before.

He doesn't condemn you here. He just tells you the truth. And if you stay still long enough, that truth will set you free.

It feels as if He's preparing the room for surgery. The air is cold. The light is bright. Everything false has been stripped away. I'm not healed yet, but I can sense the presence of the Physician. The hands that are going to cut are also the hands that are going to mend. And for the first time in a long time, I'm not fighting them.

The Near-Death Moment

There's a kind of quiet that comes after you stop talking. Not peace, not yet, but a silence that feels heavy, as if the air itself is holding its breath.

I remember the night it all caught up to me. I had reached the end of my explanations, the end of my clever fixes. Every prayer sounded recycled. Every thought felt tired. I sat in a small room lit by a single lamp, the kind of light that makes everything look softer and sadder at the same time. The clock on the wall ticked louder than it should have. I remember thinking how strange it is that a sound that steady can make you feel so empty.

I whispered, *God, I can't fix this. I can't fix me.*

It didn't feel like faith. It felt like defeat.

Even then, I don't think I was ready to let go. I was still hoping God might give me a shortcut, a gentler path. I wanted healing without the surgery.

It might sound dramatic, but I think dying to yourself often looks painfully ordinary. It's not some epic spiritual moment with thunder and lightning. It looks like running out of energy to perform. It looks like finally sitting still when every instinct in you is screaming to get up and try one more time. It looks like staring at your phone but not calling anyone, because you don't have the words anymore. It looks like standing in the shower longer than you need to because at least the water is warm and you don't have to think. It looks like realizing that all your striving, all your hustling, all your trying to fix yourself and manage everyone's perception of you has only led you right back to the same room, the same chair, the same silence you've been running from for years.

For years I had skimmed over a verse in John without really letting it land: "Unless a grain of wheat falls into the earth and dies, it remains alone; but if it dies, it bears much fruit" (John 12:24). I had always read that as a nice poetic metaphor. You know, something Jesus said to make a point. That night it felt literal. As though I could feel it in my chest. I was the seed, still clinging to the surface, terrified of what would happen if I let go and fell into the soil. Terrified of the dark. Terrified of being buried. Terrified that if I actually died to myself, there might not be anything left.

I could see what needed to die. Pride. Control. The need to be right in every argument. The quiet belief that I could earn my own peace if I just worked hard enough, prayed long enough, served enough people, fixed enough problems. I could see it all clearly, as if someone had turned on every light in the house. But I wasn't ready to let it go. Seeing isn't the same as surrendering. Knowing what needs to die and actually letting it die are two very different things.

That's the hardest part of transformation, I think. You recognize what has to die. You can name it. You can talk about it in therapy or with a trusted friend. But your hands just won't open. You're still holding on. Still white-knuckling it. Still convincing yourself that maybe, just maybe, you can keep this one thing and still be whole.

It feels like standing at the edge of something vast, staring down into the dark. You want to trust the fall, but everything in you is screaming to back away.

In that silence, I sensed the same presence I had felt earlier in the cave. It wasn't distant. It felt close. Patient. Almost tender. The Physician. I could picture Him there, waiting beside the table. The instruments ready. The light steady. But He wouldn't move without permission. Healing never happens by force.

I sat there, caught between exhaustion and resistance. I wish I could say I surrendered that night. I didn't. Not fully. I still held on to a few things, small pieces of control I didn't know how to release yet.

But something shifted. For the first time, I stopped trying to manage my own recovery. I stopped telling God what I needed and just sat there with nothing left to say. Maybe that's where death actually begins. It's in the pause between words, in the moment when striving finally runs out of breath.

Every story reaches a point when the main character stops fighting. Not because he or she wants to lose, but because the realization that winning was never the goal has come. That night was my point of stillness.

It didn't feel sacred. It didn't even feel hopeful. It felt like the end of me.

But now, when I look back, I know that was the beginning of something new.

The cave grew darker, but the darkness wasn't empty. It was full of quiet waiting.

The Edge of the Tomb

I have always imagined the tomb as a place of finality, but lately I have started to wonder if it might be a waiting room. Not the kind with bad lighting and old magazines, but the kind where time itself slows down, where breath becomes prayer, and all that is left to do is nothing.

I used to think resurrection happened in an instant, but maybe it begins quietly. Maybe it starts here, in this pause between what has ended and what has not yet begun.

It occurred to me that death isn't the hardest part. Waiting is.

I could still feel the weight of everything I had confessed, all the truth I had faced, but there was also a strange stillness in it. The striving had stopped. The noise had faded. I felt emptied out, but in a way that wasn't hopeless.

He "emptied himself," the Scriptures say of Jesus (Philippians 2:7).

I thought about that. About how He let go of every right, every claim, every defense. I could almost hear the words echo in the quiet: *He emptied Himself; I am still full of myself.*

There, on the edge of the tomb, that truth landed like a whisper.

I am beginning to understand that God doesn't lead us to this place to crush us. He brings us here to show us our limits. He brings us here because resurrection makes sense only to those who have reached the end of their own strength.

Psalm 139:8 (NIV) says, "If I make my bed in the depths, you are there." I used to imagine those depths as something to escape from. Like a pit you climb out of as fast as you can. But now I see them differently. God isn't waiting for me on the other side of this darkness, standing at the exit with His arms crossed, tapping His foot. He's here in it. Right here. In the stillness. In the soil. In the silence that follows surrender. In the mess. In the doubt. In the moments when I'm not even sure I believe anymore.

It feels like mercy that He doesn't rush this part. He lets me linger here long enough to see that what I've been calling death is actually the doorway to life. He's not hurrying me through. He's not annoyed that I'm taking so long. He's just here. Present. Patient. Waiting with me.

Sometimes I picture Jesus in His tomb. Not as a symbol or a sermon illustration, but as a real man whose lungs had stopped. Whose body was still and cold. Whose followers had already started grieving and going back to their old lives because they thought it was over. Everything looked finished. Done. The end of the story. Yet in that stillness, something was happening. Something unseen. Something holy. Something irreversible. The kind of work that happens only in the dark and the quiet when no one's watching.

Maybe that's what this edge feels like. You can't see it happening, but you can sense it somehow. Something deep in you knows the story isn't over. You can't explain it. You can't prove it. But there's this tiny flicker of something that won't let you completely give up.

I don't know how long this waiting lasts. It might be different for each of us. Some people linger here for days. Others for months. Some for years. But if you're in that space right now, don't rush it. Don't let anyone tell you to hurry up and get over it. The tomb isn't empty yet, but it will be. That's the promise. It will be.

This is where surrender becomes trust. This is where love begins to do its work in the dark, in the places you can't see or control or manage.

I'm learning that the tomb isn't where God leaves you. It's where He meets you. The tomb is quiet now. Not silent, exactly. There's a faint hum of life somewhere beneath it all, like a heartbeat you can barely hear. But it's quiet enough that I can finally hear myself breathe.

I am still here. Not fixed, not finished, just here. And maybe that's the miracle already beginning.

I used to think faith was about strength, about doing the right thing even when it hurt. Now I think faith begins when you stop pretending to be strong. It grows in weakness. It takes root in surrender. It comes alive in the space where your own power runs out.

Sometimes I still wonder how long this waiting will last. Part of me wants to rush it, to climb out of the cave and prove I am whole. But there's another part, a smaller, quieter part, that knows the story is not supposed to end with my effort.

The longer I sit here, the more I realize that resurrection is not something I can make happen. It comes when it comes.

Here's my prayer in the dark and quiet, which you can make your prayer too:

Lord, I see the pride. I see the offense. I see the parts of me that still hurt others. Give me courage to face what I cannot fix.

You are not asking me to perform. You are asking me to yield. You are not demanding perfection. You are waiting for permission.

Maybe that is the secret I have missed all along. Healing doesn't happen when I try harder. It happens when I stop running from Your hands.

The light that reaches me here is faint, but it is real. It is not the flood of morning yet, but it is enough to see that You are near.

I am standing at the edge of the tomb now, and I can feel the air begin to move. Something is shifting, something I cannot control or explain. It feels like the start of a heartbeat.

I have not stepped out yet, but the stone is not as heavy as it was.

The next breath will cost me everything.

What the Cave Reveals

You have followed me this far into the cave. By now, the air has thinned. The noise of the world has faded. And what remains is only you, your heart, and God's presence pressing in close.

This is where many turn back. It is one thing to talk about surrender; it is another to live it. But if you stay here, still, honest, and open, Scripture promises that something sacred will happen.

Let's take a look at three kinds of places the cave can be in our lives.

1. The cave as the place of exposure

The Word of God does not flatter us. It reveals us. Hebrews 4:12 says, "For the word of God is living and active, sharper than any two-edged sword, piercing to the division of soul and of spirit, of joints and of marrow, and discerning the thoughts and intentions of the heart."

That verse may sound intimidating, but it describes exactly what happens in this part of the journey. God's Word becomes the scalpel in the hands of the Great Physician. It cuts, but only to heal. It pierces, but only to separate what is false from what is true.

Notice how the verse ends: "discerning the thoughts and intentions of the heart." God is not just addressing what you do. He is revealing why you do it. The heart's motives are His focus.

If your prayers feel uncomfortable or even invasive lately, that may be what's happening. The Word is doing its work, exposing motives, separating lies from truth, dividing what you have built from what He is building in you.

Let Him work. Stay on the table.

2. The cave as the place of humility

When David cried out in Psalm 51, he was already in his own cave. His sin was exposed, his pride was shattered, his illusions of control were gone. And yet he prayed, "The sacrifices of God are a broken spirit; a broken and contrite heart, O God, you will not despise" (verse 17).

God does not despise your breaking. He receives it. In fact, brokenness is the only offering that truly reaches Him. The world teaches you to perform strength; God asks for truth.

Humility is not thinking less of yourself; it is seeing yourself clearly before a holy God and trusting that His mercy is bigger than your mistakes.

Paul calls us to examine ourselves when, in the New Covenant, we take Communion. Self-examination is not about shame, but about honesty before God. We look inward, recognizing our sin, so it doesn't quietly poison our souls. This moment calls for humility, repentance, and transparency.

At Passover, the focus was not on imperfection or self-critique. The worshipers were told to look at the lamb and see only its perfection. The spotlight was on the sacrifice, not the sinner. With Christ, both realities come together. In Communion, we honestly observe our need for grace, and at the same time we lift our eyes to behold Jesus as our perfect substitute. He is the Lamb who takes away our sin.

This table is no longer a place of condemnation, but a place of healing. When our eyes turn to Christ, Communion transforms us. We move from brokenness to wholeness by trusting in His perfection to cover every part of us. That is the miracle of grace.

3. The cave as the place of new desire

In John 12:24, Jesus said, "Unless a grain of wheat falls into the earth and dies, it remains alone; but if it dies, it bears much fruit."

That verse is not about loss. It is about transformation. The seed does not disappear; it becomes something new.

God never buries what He cannot resurrect.

If you are in a cave season, it may feel as though your story is over. But Scripture shows that the soil of surrender is where new roots begin. You are not being buried. You are being planted.

Sitting with What God Is Showing You

Take a moment before you move on. Sit with what God has been showing you. Ask yourself:

What truth is God revealing about my heart right now?

Where am I still trying to control what only He can heal?

What part of me feels as if it's dying—and what might God be preparing to resurrect in its place?

What would it mean for me to stay on the table and let the Great Physician finish what He started?

Again, don't rush this process. As I said earlier about Joshua, it takes courage not only to face the future but to face the past. Let the Surgeon open the chambers of your heart and expose some areas that have needed healing for a long time.

You can trust that you will come out of the cave, back into the light, much healthier and more whole than when you went in. Make my prayer on the operating table your prayer too:

Father, I confess that I do not always trust Your process. I want to be healed, but I still flinch when You reach for the places that hurt. Today, I choose to stay still under Your hand. Search me. Heal me. Remove what cannot remain. I believe You are not burying me; You are planting me. In Jesus' name, Amen.

7

resurrection of the heart

William was in his late forties and in good shape. He worked out, ate relatively well, and kept up with his annual checkups. Each year he had lab work done, but this year, his wife wanted him to get a certain test, a coronary calcium scan, to make sure his arteries were clear and healthy.

The physician who read the scan noticed something unusual. The numbers were fine and the arteries were clean, but something deeper was wrong. A shadow on the scan. A shape that didn't belong.

William was lifting weights in the gym the next day when the doctor's office called and told him to come in immediately. The caller added, "And please don't lift anything heavier than twenty pounds in the meantime!"

He racked the heavy barbell (yes, he was lifting as much weight as he was capable of when he received the call), a feeling of fear beginning to creep in.

"William," the doctor said later that day in the office, "you have an aneurysm."

The word confused him. He had only ever heard it in connection with the brain. "What?" he asked.

"It's an upper thoracic aortic aneurysm," the doctor explained. "It's a miracle we found it. Most people never know they have one until it ruptures and kills them. We need to operate as soon as possible."

The doctor wasn't a believer, but even he called it a miracle that they had detected it.

William had no symptoms, no warning signs, nothing to alert him that something deadly was quietly developing inside him. He recalled hearing about people with an aneurysm dropping dead on the spot when it became too late.

Only 28 days later, he was being prepped for open-heart surgery. The sterile smell of the hospital filled his nose as he signed the final consent forms. Monitors beeped in the background. A nurse clipped sensors to his chest. When the anesthesiologist asked if he was ready, William hesitated. How do you ever get ready to have your chest opened and your heart exposed?

He was about to enter a different kind of cave than we talked about in the previous chapter. Not the one of metaphor or prayer, but a literal one. Cold, sterile, lit by fluorescent light instead of faith.

As he was beginning to count backward into anesthetic oblivion, one thought passed through his mind. William, the consummate do-it-yourselfer, thought, *Here's one thing I can't fix. . . .*

That's where resurrection begins. The moment you realize you are helpless and you need a physician.

A Sacred Helplessness

What we're doing right now isn't theory. It's not a Bible study or a self-help exercise. It's surgery. We're on that table, counting backward, waiting for heart surgery—finally allowing the Great Physician to come in and clear the chambers.

There's something sacred about that space between helplessness and healing. The room grows still. You hear the hum of the machines. The shuffle of unseen feet. The slow rhythm of your own breath. The monitors pulse steadily above you, but you know that control has completely left your hands. You can't get up. You can't call it off. You can't manage the process or negotiate the terms. That's where the Great Physician meets you. Not when you're strong and put together, but when you finally stop pretending that you are.

Jesus once said, "It is not the healthy who need a doctor, but the sick" (Matthew 9:12 NIV). I used to read that as a soft metaphor. A kind of gentle invitation. As though He were just being nice and inclusive. But lately, it sounds like something way more literal. He's not a counselor with a clipboard, asking how you feel. He's not a life coach with a ten-step plan to help you actualize your potential. He's the Surgeon. He opens you up. He doesn't polish what's broken or put a Band-Aid on what's infected. He removes what's killing you. He cuts out what needs to go, even when it hurts, even when you've grown attached to it.

You need to understand that He won't force it. He waits. He waits until you're tired enough, desperate enough, honest enough to finally admit that you can't fix yourself. That all your trying and striving and self-improvement projects haven't worked. That you're still stuck. Still bleeding. Still carrying the same pain you swore you had left behind.

If you've ever been in that place, lying flat and completely powerless, you know how sacred helplessness can actually feel. It's terrifying, yes. But there's also this strange peace that comes when you finally stop fighting. Resurrection doesn't begin when light bursts through the tomb in some dramatic moment. It begins on the table, in the quiet, when you finally let the Surgeon do His work.

And He starts with the chambers that hurt the most to open. The ones you've been guarding for years. The ones that hold the pain you swore you'd never revisit. The ones you've kept locked and buried because looking at them felt too dangerous, too overwhelming, too much.

Chamber of Expectations Surgery

This chamber runs on a quiet engine of disappointment. It's the place where every unmet hope, every broken promise, every prayer that seemed to bounce off the ceiling gets stored and filed away. You may not even realize how full this chamber is until something small triggers a flood—a friend's promotion, a delayed answer, a plan that falls apart for the hundredth time. Beneath the frustration is a deeper ache: the belief that God owes you a certain kind of life, and He hasn't delivered.

Expectations are tricky because they often start out holy. You believed God for something good. You prayed with faith. You stepped out in obedience. And when the outcome didn't match the picture in your head, something quietly shifted inside. Trust didn't collapse all at once. It eroded, one disappointment at a time, until you stopped expecting anything at all—or worse, started expecting the worst. You still show up on Sundays. You still read your Bible. But there's a wall between you and hope that wasn't always there.

When the Great Physician enters this chamber, He doesn't argue with your disappointment. He doesn't dismiss it or quote Romans 8:28 like a bandage over a broken bone: "And we know that for those who love God all things work together for good." He sits with you in it. He lets you grieve what never came. He lets you say what you've been afraid to say: that it hurt, that you're tired, that you don't understand why He didn't come through the way you thought He would.

And then, slowly, He begins to untangle your expectations from His promises. You start to see that He never promised comfort on your terms. He promised presence. He never promised a pain-free life. He promised a redeemed one. The surgery here isn't removing your ability to hope. It's teaching your heart to anchor its hope in the character of God rather than in the outcomes you've been demanding. When that shift takes root, peace starts growing in the exact place where bitterness used to live.

Chamber of Justice Surgery

If the chamber of expectations runs on disappointment, this chamber runs on rage. It's the scorekeeping chamber, the one that remembers every wrong done to you and replays it on a loop. Someone lied. Someone cheated. Someone got away with it. And deep inside, a voice keeps whispering, *That isn't fair*. You may have forgiven with your mouth, but the chamber of justice still holds the receipt.

The wound here isn't just pain. It's injustice. It's the feeling that the scales are unbalanced and nobody seems to care. You watched someone get rewarded for what should have cost that person everything. You saw the guilty walk free while you carried the consequences. That kind of wound doesn't just hurt—it hardens. It turns the heart into a courtroom where you are simultaneously the plaintiff, the judge, and the executioner. And the verdict is always the same: *guilty*.

When the Great Physician opens this chamber, the first thing He does is disarm you. Not with force, but with a mirror. He lets you see how tightly you've been gripping the gavel—and how much it has been costing you. The bitterness you thought was protecting you has actually been poisoning you. The justice you've been demanding has kept you chained to the very person or people you wanted to be free from.

He doesn't ask you to pretend a hurt or injustice didn't happen. He doesn't tell you the offense was small. He tells you the truth: that vengeance belongs to Him, not to you (see Romans 12:19). And He shows you the cross—the place where the greatest injustice in history became the greatest act of mercy. When you finally release the case you've been building against someone, your hands don't feel empty. They feel free. Mercy doesn't enter this chamber as weakness. It enters as liberation. And when it does, the walls that rage built begin to come down.

Chamber of Confidence Surgery

The issue here is hard to find because this chamber looks so healthy. It hides behind competence and control. You are good at what you do. You take care of your people. You keep things moving. You've built a reputation on reliability. People come to you for advice. They trust you to get things done. They may even admire your calm and consistency. But beneath the surface, there is a quiet panic: *If I stop performing, will I still be worth anything?*

That question hums beneath almost everything. It drives the extra hours no one asked you for. It keeps you awake long after the work is finished. It makes rest feel unsafe, as if stopping might cause everything to collapse. It disguises itself as diligence, but deep down, it's fear. The fear of being ordinary. The fear of being unseen.

You tell yourself you're demonstrating responsibility or leadership or stewardship. You even quote that verse about working as unto the Lord. But sometimes that verse becomes a shield to hide behind. You start to confuse obedience with obsession. What began as devotion slowly turns into dependence on achievement. You call it excellence, but it's often anxiety dressed as virtue.

This chamber beats to the rhythm of "one more." One more project, one more compliment, one more success to prove that you belong. You might even call that drive passion or calling. But somewhere along the way, the good desire to serve has been hijacked by the fear of insignificance. You don't feel free to stop, because your worth is tied to your output.

When the Great Physician enters this chamber, He doesn't begin with pressure or pain. He begins with silence. He lets things slow down until the noise that once kept you alive begins to fade. A plan fails. A season ends. The phone stops ringing. At first it feels like loss, but it's really an invitation to listen. The stillness you used to avoid begins to reveal the truth. The world does not need your constant effort to keep spinning.

As things quiet, you begin to notice how much of your identity has been wrapped around your usefulness. It appears in small moments. You feel guilty for resting. You apologize for saying no. You measure your prayers by their productivity. It begins to dawn on you that the same drive that made you successful has also made you restless.

God is not trying to take away your strength. He is trying to untangle your worth from it. He wants you to know that you are not His employee, but His child. The gifts He gave you were never meant to replace intimacy with Him. They were meant to flow from it.

At first, this realization feels like something breaking. You look at what you've built and wonder if it mattered. You question whether you've wasted your energy chasing approval that never satisfied you. Yet even in the ache, something sacred begins to grow. You start to feel God's pleasure again—not because you've done something to earn it, but because you've stopped running long enough to feel it.

The noise quiets. The striving slows. You begin to see your work differently. It becomes worship rather than worthiness. You can work hard without being driven by fear. You can lead without needing to control. You can rest without guilt.

In that stillness, confidence returns, but it is different. It no longer depends on applause or results. It no longer rises and falls with how others perceive you. It is steady and rooted in presence, in the quiet assurance that God's pleasure does not fluctuate with your performance.

This is not the confidence of control. It is the confidence of belonging. It is what Jesus carried when He stepped into the Jordan River before performing a single miracle and heard the Father say that He was a beloved Son with whom He was well pleased (see Matthew 3:17). That same voice speaks to you now. It reminds you that your worth was settled long before your first success and will remain long after your last.

When that truth takes root, the need to prove yourself begins to fade. The rest you once resisted becomes sacred. The silence no longer feels empty. It feels full. And the heart that once raced to be seen now beats in rhythm with peace.

Chamber of Memory Surgery

This is the oldest and most fragile chamber. The air feels heavy here. Every wound, every regret, every betrayal just lingers in these walls. Some memories are still sharp and recent. Others are faded, tucked away for years. You don't visit this place often, but it visits you. A certain smell, a song on the radio, someone's voice—any of it can swing that door wide open without any warning.

You've tried to close it. You tell yourself the past is the past, that you've moved on. But memory is unbelievably stubborn. It waits for the quiet moments. It shows up in your dreams. It leaks out through your reactions when you least expect it. You find yourself snapping over something small, and you know, you *know*, it's because something way deeper still hasn't healed.

The chamber of memory is where your heart stores everything it couldn't make sense of at the time. The mistakes you made. The people you lost. The moments you'd give anything to rewrite. It's like a museum of unfinished stories, and every single thing in there whispers the same painful question: *Where were You, God?*

When God starts working in this chamber, He doesn't lead with answers. He starts with just showing up. He doesn't erase what happened. He steps into it. He walks those corridors of memory right next to you, reaching out to touch what you were sure was too broken to ever fix. There are places where He stops and lingers, not to dig the wound open again, but quietly to remind you that He was actually there all along.

At first, you resist it. It feels so much easier just to leave the door shut. But eventually, you realize that avoiding your memories hasn't actually protected you from anything. It's only kept you from understanding what they were trying to show you. You start to see that healing doesn't come from forgetting. It comes from finally letting God step into the story with you.

And then something starts to shift. Some memories begin to change shape under His light. That betrayal that used to define everything about you? It becomes the ground where real compassion starts to grow. That loss that carved you out and left you hollow? It becomes the space where empathy can finally take root. That pain that made you so bitter for so long? It becomes the story that now makes people actually believe you when you talk about God. You start to see what Joseph saw when he looked at his brothers and said, "You meant it for evil. But God meant it for good" (see Genesis 50:20).

The hardest memories to face, however, are those where you're the one who caused the damage. The words you can't take back. The years you threw away. The people you should have loved better, but didn't. These memories sting in a different way because they come with guilt attached. But even here, even with these, God doesn't condemn you. He reminds you that grace isn't just a nice idea or a Bible word. It's real. It happened. The cross is His answer to every single moment you wish you could go back and undo.

Healing in this chamber takes time. Real time. It doesn't happen in one powerful prayer or one breakthrough moment. It comes through being honest. Through crying. Through finally having the courage to look at what you've been running from.

The anesthesia is grace. The scalpel is mercy. And even though it aches for a while, slowly the meaning starts to change.

One day you wake up and realize something's different. The memory is still there. It didn't disappear. But it doesn't control you anymore. It doesn't get to decide who you are. It becomes something almost sacred—a scar that tells the story of how you survived. You can think about it without getting dragged back into it. You can tell someone what happened without drowning in it all over again. The wound that almost killed you becomes your strongest witness.

When this chamber finally starts to clear, when the air finally shifts, the whole room feels still. You can breathe deeply again. Gratitude starts pushing out the shame. The sorrow is still there, but now it's mixed with something that actually feels like peace. You realize that what was meant to destroy you has somehow made you deeper. More real. You start to understand that redemption was never about God hitting delete on your story. It's about Him stepping into the center of it and rewriting the ending.

The past stops feeling like this dangerous thing waiting to hurt you. It starts to feel like proof. Like a testimony. Every scar becomes a place where you can point to it and say, "That's where grace found me." And your heart, the one that used to be so weighed down with all these painful, unfinished stories, starts beating with this quiet, steady confidence: Not one of them was wasted.

Jesus: Model and Surgeon

Every surgeon works from a model, an ideal he or she is trying to restore. Surgeons study what healthy tissue is supposed to look like so they can recognize when something's wrong. In the same way, Jesus isn't just the one who heals your heart. He's the picture of what a whole heart actually looks like.

Jesus lived with every chamber open and working the way it was meant to. His expectations weren't built on comfort or success or getting what He wanted. They were rooted in His Father's will. His sense of justice was wrapped up in mercy. His confidence came from knowing exactly who He was and whose He was. And His memory, even of betrayal and pain, wasn't poisoned by bitterness or resentment.

When people misunderstood Jesus, He didn't hit back. When they abandoned Him, He didn't shut down and pull away. When they nailed Him to a cross, He prayed for the ones holding the hammer. The human heart had never beaten like that before.

That's why His resurrection was more than just proof He was God. It was the blueprint. It showed us what restored humanity actually looks like. The heart that used to be chained to offense, fear, and pride can now live like His heart.

But to become like Him, we've got to go where He went. Before the resurrection came surrender. Before the glory came the cut.

In Gethsemane, Jesus said, "Not my will, but yours, be done" (Luke 22:42).Those words aren't poetic or pretty. They're surgical. They cut through that final layer of resistance. They expose the deepest truth of what it means to live with a heart that can't be offended anymore, trusting that even when the Father's will is painful right now, it's leading somewhere good. Ask yourself:

What would it look like for me to lay myself on the Surgeon's table and trust that the result will be healing, even with the scars?

Am I ready to surrender to the Father's will and let Him lay bare the painful chambers of my heart so I can be made whole?

On the cross, Jesus was laid completely bare and literally pierced. His heart was opened up. And out of that wound came blood and water, the very symbols of cleansing and new birth. The Surgeon Himself took the incision so that every one of us could survive ours.

When He rose again, He didn't hide the scars. He showed them off. He invited Thomas to actually touch the place where the spear went in, as if He was saying, "This is what healing looks like. Not the absence of pain, but the presence of peace."

That's the pattern for resurrection: surrender, incision, healing, and then life that never ends.

Sometimes I think we really underestimate how radical that pattern is. We want the empty tomb without the garden of surrender. The joy without the dying. But the only way to get a resurrected heart is through the surrender of every single chamber.

And once you've been through that kind of surgery, you start recognizing it in other people. The ones who have let God open them up are just different. There's this gentleness that doesn't come from being weak. There's this courage that doesn't need to be loud or prove anything. Others who have gone under the same Surgeon's knife carry peace the way healed skin carries a scar—not hidden away, but holy.

That's the life Jesus modeled, and it's the one He's still performing in everyone who trusts Him. The Great Physician doesn't just heal hearts. He trains them to beat like His.

8

surrender is not a sidenote

Every resurrection looks a little different, but the pattern is always the same. Something dies. Something gets surrendered. And then, quietly, life starts up again.

Imagine a man who's been carrying bitterness toward his father for most of his adult life. The wound runs deep. His dad was harsh, impossible to please, and that pain became the lens through which this man looked at every relationship. His heart learned to stay locked up tight.

One night, after years of acting as though he were fine, the man finally admits he is not. He writes his father's name on a scrap of paper, prays through tears, and asks God to help him forgive. The next week, he picks up the phone. The conversation is awkward and short. There is no big, dramatic moment. No tearful apology. But afterward, he sits in his car and just exhales. For the first time in years, he can actually breathe again. That's resurrection. The return of peace to a heart that had completely forgotten how to rest.

Or picture a woman who has spent her whole life trying to keep everyone happy. Every choice, every sentence, every decision gets filtered through her inner question, *What will they think?* On the outside, she looks composed and put together. On the inside, she's completely exhausted.

One day, this woman realizes that her constant need for approval isn't humility. It's fear. She prays this simple, honest prayer: *Lord, I'm so tired of needing everyone to like me*. Change doesn't happen overnight. But something starts to shift. She starts saying no when she actually needs to. She starts reading her Bible not to earn points, but just to hear God's voice. Over time, she starts feeling like herself again. That's what happens when the chamber of confidence finally heals. The heart stops performing and starts living.

Or think about a pastor who has spent years preaching about grace, while secretly being unable to receive it himself. A long time ago, a moral failure broke something deep inside him. He repented. He rebuilt his life. But the shame still hangs around like a shadow that won't leave. He believes God forgives him. Intellectually, he knows it. But he just can't seem to forgive himself.

One day in prayer, this pastor stops asking God to make him feel better and just asks for one thing: *Help me actually believe that Christ's blood really is enough*. Slowly, something lifts. When he stands up to preach again, his words sound different. They carry this weight, this tenderness, this freedom he didn't have before. That's resurrection too. The chamber of memory finally cleared out and filled with mercy instead.

These stories aren't unusual. They happen quietly, usually without anyone watching, but they're real. The Great Physician is still working. He opens up what's diseased, cuts out what's dead, and somehow restores what we were sure was gone forever. The heart He gives back is never quite the same as the one we handed Him. It's stronger. Softer. More alive.

That's the promise of the resurrected heart. It keeps beating with His rhythm, even after it has been completely broken.

Practical Surrender

After you've handed the Surgeon your whole heart, when it starts beating again, there is a strange stillness that follows. You feel alive, but also exposed. The air in the room is heavier, charged with something holy. You realize that you have just lived through something you did not understand and could not control.

Only then do the questions come: *Why did He ask for my surrender? Why did He need me to let go?*

Because surrender is not a sidenote in the Christian life. It's the center of it.

We talk about faith as if it were belief, but faith without surrender is just admiration. It costs nothing. Surrender is where faith turns into love. It is where trust stops being theoretical and becomes embodied.

That's why Jesus asked it of every person He ever called. "Follow Me," He said. Not "agree with Me." Not "respect Me." *Follow.* The Greek word for follow, *akoloutheō*, means to walk the same road.[1] It is the language of motion, of leaving behind. When Jesus called the fishermen, they dropped their nets. When He called Matthew, he left his tax booth. When He called you, He meant for you to lay something down too.

There is no resurrection without surrender. There never has been.

Paul describes it in Philippians 2:8–9 (NIV): "He humbled himself by becoming obedient to death—even death on a cross! Therefore God exalted him." The word *therefore* is small but crucial. It means one thing flows from another. Exaltation follows surrender. Power follows humility. Glory follows obedience.

They always have.

We want the resurrection without the cross, the joy without the incision, the life without the loss. But there is no shortcut.

Jesus Himself went through the full surgery. He wasn't just the Physician; He was the patient. His heart was pierced first.

In Gethsemane, He faced His own table. The stone was cold beneath Him. The night air hung thick with silence. The moonlight fell through the olive branches, and the shadows trembled like hands. His friends were only a few feet away, but they were asleep. The kind of sleep that comes when sorrow is too heavy to bear awake.

Jesus was alone.

He knelt in the dirt in agony, knowing what was coming. The betrayal. The mockery. The nails. The devastating moment when His Father would turn His face away for the only time in eternal history. Every breath Jesus drew tasted like death. Scripture says He began to sweat drops of blood, and doctors tell us that's not metaphor, but a rare physical condition that occurs under the most extreme stress imaginable. The body literally leaks blood through the sweat glands when the pressure inside becomes unbearable.

That was His body breaking under the weight of the sin of the world, before the cross even touched it.

And then, our Lord prayed the most honest prayer ever recorded: "Father, if you are willing, take this cup from me" (Luke 22:42 NIV).

Those staggering words are not weakness. They are truth.

That prayer carries the entire weight of human fear and divine obedience in the same breath. It is the sound of a heart cracking open.

Jesus paused there. Maybe for a long, long time. At that late hour, the Garden was silent except for the sound of His breathing, the rustle of leaves, the distant city lights flickering through the trees. Jesus could have stood up. He could have called the angels. He could have walked away and left the world to its own judgment, the judgment it deserved.

But He stayed. Maybe there was a long, long pause . . .

And then He spoke the words that would change everything.

"Yet . . .

. . . not my will, but yours be done."

And it was done. The surrender was complete, and heaven and earth would now move toward the fulfillment of thousands of years of prophecy.

Friends, that's not poetic language. It is surgical. It is the moment the Son of God gives consent. The greatest heart ever to live, lying open before the Father. The incision made, not by nails, not yet, but by surrender.

In that moment, heaven held its breath. The angels who had served Him since creation watched the Son of God willingly submit Himself to the Father's will.

But what you and I have to understand is that He was not losing power. He was using it.

That's what surrender really is. Power placed under love. Control laid down in trust. The Son saying to the Father, "Cut as deep as You must. I am Yours."

And from that open heart, the Great Physician learned the art of healing ours.

Surrender is terrifying because it feels like death. And in a way, it is. It's the death of self-will, of control, of an illusion that we know better than God.

But it's also the doorway to life. Jesus didn't just endure surrender; He embodied it.

The reason He can perform surgery on us is that He underwent it Himself. That's what Hebrews means when it says, "We do not have a high priest who is unable to empathize with our weaknesses, but we have one who has been tempted in every way, just as we are—yet he did not sin" (Hebrews 4:15 NIV). He knows what it feels like to tremble, to sweat blood, to whisper, *Is there any other way?* and still say yes.

That is why we can trust Him.

For us, surrender is not a onetime act. It's a rhythm. A pattern that repeats. You lay one thing down, breathe again, and then He invites you to lay something else down. Each time, a little more control dies, and a little more of His life fills the empty space.

For years, I would buy a Father's Day card and anonymously drop it in the mailbox. It was my attempt to send the longings of my broken heart into the void of rejection, as if some mysterious reply would one day come. I didn't have a relationship with my biological father. I tried, yet it wasn't reciprocated. Like my Father's Day cards, each bid for intimacy was trapped in an endless cycle of nondelivery.

The last time I spoke with him was on the phone, on my 21st birthday. I asked one final time if we could have a relationship, and he simply replied, "Let sleeping dogs lie."

The conversation ended, as did any expectation of building a relationship. A few years later, I received the news that he had died. My initial thought: *How can I ever forgive him now that he's gone?* This revealed how little I understood about forgiveness.

It was years later, when my wife revealed that she had kept a record of my wrongs in that leather-bound notebook, when she decided to throw the notebook away, release all tangible proof that it had ever happened, and forgive me fully—without me even asking or formally apologizing—that I understood how I could forgive my father after he had passed away. My wife taught me one of life's greatest lessons. She taught me that my heart could be free, even if other people never say the right thing.

When you watch Jesus, you start to see that every miracle He did came from a surrendered heart. He never acted on impulse or out of pride. He never said something just to win an argument or prove He was right. Over and over, He said, "I only do what I see the Father doing." That wasn't weakness. That wasn't passivity. That was power living under authority.

His entire life was built on surrender. In fact, His incarnation might have been the first surrender. Before Gethsemane. Before Calvary. There was that moment when the eternal Son of God chose to take on flesh. Paul describes it in Philippians 2:6–9:

> Though he was in the form of God, [he] did not count equality with God a thing to be grasped, but emptied himself, by taking the form of a servant, being born in the likeness of men. And being found in human form, he humbled himself by becoming obedient to the point of death, even death on a cross. Therefore God has highly exalted him and bestowed on him the name that is above every name.

That phrase "emptied himself" carries way more weight than our language can even hold. The Greek word is *kenoō*—to pour out, to make yourself nothing.[2] It wasn't a loss of His divinity. It was the laying aside of privilege. The Son, who had spoken entire galaxies into being, chose to become bound by time, by hunger, by the fragility of human skin. The one who had never experienced need let Himself need things. That was surrender long before the cross ever happened.

The same passage says He humbled Himself by "becoming obedient," and the Greek word Paul uses there, *hupakoē*, means to listen under.[3] It's this picture of someone leaning in close, waiting for the next word, ready to move the second the Father speaks. That's what obedience looks like in its purest form. Not forced compliance. Not gritting your teeth and doing what you're told. But intimate trust.

That kind of obedience isn't weakness. It's actually the highest form of strength there is. It's spiritual authority at its fullest. When the heart fully surrenders, heaven starts to move through it.

Maybe that's actually the hardest truth to accept. We spend our whole lives trying to become strong, trying to hold it all together, trying to control the outcomes. But in the Kingdom of God, strength works backward. You don't gain power by tightening your grip. You gain it by opening your hands. You don't become resilient by hardening your heart. You become resilient by letting it stay soft.

Every incision of surrender reveals a deeper kind of freedom. Every yes opens up another chamber. Every act of letting go creates space for the breath of God to come in.

So if you feel that pressure right now, if God seems to be pressing on something deep inside you, don't fight it. That pressure isn't punishment. It's an invitation. It means the Great Physician is close.

And on the other side of surrender is resurrection. Always.

The Great Exchange

Are you sweating blood yet?

That's where every true surrender begins. It was the place Jesus went before the cross, where His own sweat literally turned to blood and He prayed, "Not my will, but yours, be done." The cross didn't start on Calvary. It started in the Garden. It started in that moment when Jesus chose to trust the Father's hands more than His own will. Every real resurrection starts there too.

You might not be in a garden tonight, but you know what it feels like to kneel under the weight of a choice. You know what it feels like when God asks for something you're not sure you can give. Your heart races. Your mind argues. Your whole body trembles. You whisper that you trust Him, but everything in you wants to hold on just a little bit longer.

Every act of surrender feels like loss at first. You give up control. You let go of a right you thought you had. You stop defending something that used to define who you are. It feels like letting go of oxygen. The hands that used to clutch and grip in self-protection now tremble as they slowly open. The heart protests, not because it doesn't love God, but because it has learned to survive by holding on tight.

But in God's economy, nothing surrendered stays empty for long. The Great Physician never removes something without replacing it. What He takes out, He replaces with life. He doesn't wound just to hurt you. He wounds to heal. Every incision He makes in you is one He has already received Himself. The Great Physician became the patient. The wounds that are healing you right now are still visible in His hands. The Surgeon bears His own scars.

This is the moment when the light in the operating room shifts. It's not just analysis anymore. It's encounter. The Great Physician is standing right beside the table where your soul is laid out, calm and certain, waiting for your permission. He won't force His way in. He waits for your yes.

He doesn't need eloquence. He doesn't need you to be strong or have it all together. A simple whisper will do: *Yes, Lord. I'm ready. Do what You need to do.*

And then He begins.

Exchanging expectations for peace

When you hand Him expectations, He gives peace.

At first, the release feels small. Almost trivial. You take one situation that's been keeping you up at night and you offer it to Him. A child's future. A strained relationship. A dream that's just not going to happen. You tell Him it's His now. Then you wait, expecting something dramatic to happen. Instead, what comes is silence. But it's not the silence of nobody being there. It's the silence of rest.

Slowly, that tightness in your chest starts to ease. You don't have to run the same mental movie on repeat anymore. The future that used to feel like a constant project you had to manage becomes something you can actually trust instead of control.

Peace starts to form like a gentle tide washing over a restless shore. You notice small things again. The wind outside. The taste of your morning coffee. The laughter of someone you love. These were always gifts, but now you're finally still enough to receive them.

Peace isn't the absence of problems. It's the settled confidence that Someone else is holding the outcome. It's the deep knowing that your story is safe even when you have no idea how it ends.

Exchanging justice for mercy

When you hand Him justice, He gives mercy.

Letting go of your right to even the score feels completely impossible until you remember how He handled your justice. The cross was the great unfairness of all history. Christ absorbed what He didn't deserve so you could live free of what you did. Every single time you choose mercy, you're not denying the wrong or pretending it didn't happen. You're choosing to let God carry what was crushing you.

You remember how heavy resentment actually is. How it keeps you chained to a past that never changes. You realize that forgiveness isn't a feeling you have to wait for. It's a decision to stop drinking poison and expecting the other person to die. Mercy isn't weakness. It's the strength of Christ flowing through a heart that finally trusts God to make things right.

And something starts to shift. The person who used to live rent-free in your mind starts to lose his or her power over you. You stop rehearsing the argument in the shower. You stop needing the person to admit what he or she did. You stop waiting for justice before you can feel whole. Mercy moves in like clean air after a storm. You can breathe again. You can even pray for the one who hurt you. Not because that person deserves it, but because you're finally free enough to love without fear.

Exchanging confidence for identity

When you hand Him confidence, He gives identity.

The striving slows down. The noise of needing to prove yourself starts to fade. It's not that ambition disappears. It just changes direction. You still have passion, but now it's serving a Person instead of feeding your ego. You're not chasing applause anymore just to feel alive. You start working from love instead of for love.

It feels awkward at first. You've lived so long with applause as your pulse that silence feels totally unnatural. But slowly you realize the quiet is actually sacred. God is speaking in it. He's telling you who you really are. You're not the roles you play or the numbers you hit or the compliments you collect. You're a child of God. Already chosen. Already accepted.

Confidence starts to come back, but it has a completely different tone now. It's calm. Steady. It doesn't need an audience anymore. It doesn't depend on outcomes. You know that failure won't define you and success won't inflate you. You can work hard without being terrified of being overlooked and rest deeply without being afraid of being forgotten. That's what it means to live with a healed chamber of confidence.

Exchanging memory for redemption

When you hand Him memory, He gives redemption.

The past doesn't vanish. It changes color. The shadows fade as light starts to seep in. The painful scenes that used to rule your mind start to lose their sharp edges. You begin to see where grace was present even in the darkness. What you thought was abandonment starts to look like protection. What you called failure becomes formation.

You realize that your story isn't something to be ashamed of. It's something to steward. God has been writing through it all. The loss that hollowed you out became the space where His presence could finally dwell. The betrayal that made you so cynical became the soil where real compassion grew. The years that felt completely wasted are now the testimony that feeds other people. Ask yourself:

Where can I see traces of the Great Physician's hands in my story?

Have I ever asked God to erase something that He might actually be trying to redeem instead?

When the Great Physician redeems your story, this is the divine exchange Isaiah talked about: beauty for ashes, joy for mourning, praise for despair. Paul said it another way: "God made him who had no sin to be sin for us, so that in him we might become the righteousness of God" (2 Corinthians 5:21 NIV). He takes what's broken and gives what's whole. He takes what died and breathes it alive again.

part three

the healed heart

9

scars are signs of life

Romans 8:11 says, "The Spirit of him who raised Jesus from the dead . . . will also give life to your mortal bodies." That's not just a promise for eternity someday. It's a promise for right now. The same Spirit who rolled away the stone still raises what's fallen inside you. He breathes life into hearts that have stopped trusting, stopped forgiving, stopped hoping. The resurrection power of Christ isn't a lesson to remember. It's a heartbeat to receive.

Close your eyes for a moment. Listen for it.

That faint rhythm you hear isn't your imagination. It's grace doing what all your effort never could. It's the sound of the old life fading and the new one forming. It's the sound of blood moving again where fear had stopped it. It's the sound of a heart that was being operated on and is now waking up.

As you rise from the table, you notice how light you feel. The colors around you seem brighter somehow. The air feels clean. You find yourself less afraid of what's coming next. You start to see beauty where there used to be just pain. You start thanking God for the scars that used to embarrass you, because now you finally understand. They're not symbols of loss. They're signs of life.

Look back for a second. Trace the pattern. Every time you handed God something you thought holding on to was absolutely essential, He gave you something eternal.

When you gave Him control, He gave you peace. When you gave Him vengeance, He gave you mercy. When you gave Him striving, He gave you identity. When you gave Him regret, He gave you redemption.

This is the great exchange. Death for life. Striving for rest. Control for peace. Condemnation for freedom.

It starts the same way every single time. With open hands.

So now the Surgeon waits again, gentle and sure. His eyes hold no demand. Only invitation. He's not asking you to try harder. He's asking you to trust deeper.

Let go of what you can't keep anyway. Release what you can't fix. Surrender what you were never meant to carry in the first place. The trade won't make sense at first, but it will save you. Because the only thing safer than holding on to your life is placing it in the hands of the One who gave His life for you.

This is what surrender feels like when it finally becomes worship. The pain you feared becomes the pathway to freedom. The tears you resisted become the river that cleanses you. The incision becomes the entry point for light.

You might feel weak as you do it, but weakness has never scared Him. It's actually the place where His strength comes most alive. The moment you stop fighting the process is the moment the miracle begins.

The Great Physician steps back from the table, His hands still steady, His eyes full of joy. You can almost hear His voice saying what He has been saying from the very beginning: *Behold, I make all things new*.

And this time, you believe Him.

Because this time, the new thing He has made is you.

Scars as Signposts

William woke up in the hospital with a long incision running down his chest. A pale line sealed by neat rows of stitches. The smell of antiseptic filled the room. Machines blinked quietly beside him, keeping rhythm with the fragile miracle of his heartbeat. Every breath pulled against the tightness in his chest. Each inhale was a reminder that something inside him had been opened up.

The doctors told him, "Move slowly. Don't lift anything heavy. Don't rush the process."

He obeyed. But every shower, every accidental glance in the mirror, brought him right back to that scar.

At first, it really bothered him. He hated the way it looked. It divided his chest like some kind of mark of weakness. It felt like fragility written right into his skin. He was too young for this kind of scar.

But time started to teach what the pain couldn't.

As the weeks passed and his strength came back, the scar began to change meaning. It didn't look like a flaw anymore.

It became evidence of healing. It was proof that something inside him had been repaired, not ruined. The scar wasn't the end of his story. It was the signature of survival. He could have been dead. Killed by the thing that had been secretly growing inside him. But God had been merciful, and the secret had been discovered. Repaired. Healed. The scar would always remind him of God's mercy.

That's what scars do. They're the intersection of pain and grace. The proof that what was once torn open has now been mended. They tell the truth that we've been through something, and that something holy happened there.

Christ carried His scars too. After the resurrection, He didn't hide them. He didn't ask the Father to erase them from His glorified body. When Thomas doubted, Jesus lifted His hands and said, "Put your finger here; see my hands. Reach out your hand and put it into my side. Stop doubting and believe" (John 20:27 NIV).

The wounds that used to speak of pain became the evidence of victory. They weren't erased, because they were part of the story of redemption. The resurrected body of Christ still carried the record of what love cost. His scars didn't disfigure Him. They revealed Him. The book of Revelation even speaks of this:

> Then I saw in the right hand of him who was seated on the throne a scroll written within and on the back, sealed with seven seals. And I saw a mighty angel proclaiming with a loud voice, "Who is worthy to open the scroll and break its seals?" And no one in heaven or on earth or under the earth was able to open the scroll or to look into it, and I began to weep loudly because no one was found worthy to open the scroll or to look into it. And one of the elders said to me, "Weep no more; behold, the Lion of the tribe of Judah, the Root of David, has conquered, so that he can open the scroll and its seven seals."
>
> And between the throne and the four living creatures and among the elders I saw a *Lamb standing, as though it had been slain*, with seven horns and with seven eyes, which are the seven spirits of God sent out into all the earth.
>
> Revelation 5:1–6, emphasis added

As though it had been slain. A Lamb like that would have a scar across its throat. His scar tells the truth of His sacrifice. His love for us. And His stripes are the sign that they have healed us (see Isaiah 53:5).

Our scars tell the same kind of story. Most of them aren't visible. They live in memory and emotion, hidden in the unseen places of the soul.

Some come from rejection that still stings. Some from words that cut deeper than anyone knew. Some from betrayal or loss.

And some from that quiet ache of your own regret. Moments when you said the wrong thing. Stayed silent when you should have spoken. Or walked away when you should have stayed.

Peter knew that kind of scar. His wound wasn't on his body. It was in his conscience. He had promised loyalty and then denied the One he loved most. When the rooster crowed, Scripture says, he went out and wept bitterly. That was the sound of a man breaking open.

But after the resurrection, Jesus, the Surgeon, came looking for him. On the shore of Galilee, by a charcoal fire just like the one where Peter had denied Him, Jesus asked, "Do you love Me?" Three times. He gave Peter three chances to answer with what he had once failed to say (see John 21:15–17). With every answer, another layer of shame fell away. The scar didn't vanish, but it healed. The failure that once silenced him became the story that gave his preaching power. The man who had been paralyzed by guilt became the one who stood before thousands and declared, "God has made this Jesus, whom you crucified, both Lord and Christ" (Acts 2:36 NKJV).

That's how God redeems scars. He doesn't erase them. He heals them. He transforms them.

Have you read about Jacob?

He wrestled with God through the night, refusing to let go until he got a blessing. When morning came, God touched his hip and wrenched it out of joint.

From that day on, Jacob walked with a limp. It wasn't punishment. It was a reminder. It marked the night he stopped striving in his own strength and started walking under grace. The sun rose as he limped away, and he named the place Peniel, saying, "I saw God face to face, and yet my life was spared" (Genesis 32:30 NIV).

The limp didn't limit him. It testified.

The testimony was that he had encountered God and lived.

The same is true for us. Every wound healed in God's presence becomes a witness that we have seen Him face-to-face.

The healed heart bears its marks, but they don't throb with pain anymore. They pulse with gratitude. The fear that used to live there gets replaced with wonder. The bitterness that once filled a chamber becomes compassion for others who are still on the table. When you see people struggling with their own wound, you recognize the look. You remember what it felt like to wonder if the pain would ever end. And from that memory rises a tenderness that wasn't there before.

That's how you know the heart has truly been resurrected. It beats again not just for you, but for others. It doesn't cling to comfort anymore. It seeks out the wounded. It becomes a vessel through which healing flows.

The Great Physician doesn't heal us just to make us whole. He heals us so our lives become a signpost. A living testimony that death never gets the final word. He leaves the scar so the world can see what love has done. William's impending death was traded for a scar. This is always the case. A scar or a limp reminds us of what could have happened without the intervention of the Master Surgeon.

Every healed heart becomes a witness that pain isn't permanent and that grace never wastes a wound.

The miracle isn't that the scar fades. The miracle is that it doesn't hurt anymore. It has been repurposed. What was once a record of trauma has become a declaration of triumph.

The place that once marked your breaking now becomes your testimony.

And when you look around, you start to notice something. The people who walk with the deepest peace are often the ones who walk with scars. The ones who carry the most light are often the ones who have wrestled with God and lived. The men and women who carry the gentlest presence are the ones who have faced their darkness and let grace heal it.

They limp a little, but their eyes shine. They laugh easily and forgive quickly. They don't need to prove anything. They've already been to the end of themselves and found God waiting there. You can see it in how they listen. In how they love. In how they take their time with others. They're patient, because they remember how long healing took. They're kind, because they remember what it felt like to be broken.

You're looking at Christlikeness. A disciple who has learned from and been healed by his Master.

Such disciples are humble, because they know the difference between being strong and being sustained. And when they speak, something inside you starts to believe again. You sense that they've seen things you haven't seen and heard things only the wounded can hear.

These are the people who walk with scars and joy at the same time. They're both fragile and fierce. Their peace isn't naive. It has been tested in the fire. They've learned to live with the Holy Spirit as breath and rhythm. The presence of God isn't just something they talk about. It radiates from them.

These are the living signs of resurrection: the healed and the healing, the wounded and the worshiping, the ones whose hearts have been cut open and filled with new life. They move through the world quietly, yet everywhere they go, life begins to stir.

And if you've surrendered to surgery, that's who you are becoming too. The scar is still there as a sign, but it doesn't tell a story of pain anymore. It tells a story of power. It tells the world that love has conquered death, and it shows in the most ordinary way possible. In the joy on your face. In the peace in your eyes. In the way your presence makes others believe that hope is still alive.

Because the Great Physician has touched you. And the touch of His hand never fades.

Reflecting on Your Scars

Take a moment to thank God for the mark that remains. Ask Him to help you see your scar not as a flaw, but as a sign of His faithfulness and as a signpost for others. Ask yourself:

What scar in my life, whether emotional, spiritual, or physical, has become my greatest teacher?

How might my healed wound become a signpost and a source of healing for someone else?

Every scar tells a story, but resurrection was never meant to end with just survival. The Great Physician doesn't simply mend hearts. He mobilizes them. Once you've felt His hands on your life, you are called to carry His touch into the world. To walk among the wounded as someone who knows the way home.

The next chapter is about that movement. What happens when a resurrected heart starts to live beyond itself—joining the mission of Jesus to heal, to forgive, to restore.

Because healed people don't keep the miracle to themselves. They become it.

10

joining the mission

I talked earlier about the Hero's Journey, the ancient pattern that runs through every great story. From Moses to Frodo, from Esther to Peter, the same rhythm repeats: a call, a descent, a death, and a return. Back then, I described it as a literary device. But standing where I am now, I see it for what it really is: a road map for discipleship.

Because this isn't just myth or metaphor. It's what actually happens when God calls someone to live from the heart.

Before you can ever return, you have to leave.

I still remember my first call to adventure. It didn't come through thunder or lightning. It came through restlessness. I had what I thought I wanted: ministry success, people's approval, a sense of purpose. But it all started to feel hollow. Somewhere in that emptiness, I heard Him whisper, *There's more.*

That whisper undid me.

The call of God rarely arrives with a spotlight. It arrives as discomfort, as longing, as holy dissatisfaction. The ache for more is not ambition. It's invitation.

I didn't know it then, but that whisper was the beginning of my transformation. I tried to ignore it. I tried to stay where it was safe. But every true calling eventually requires a leaving. Abraham had to leave his country. Peter had to leave his nets. I had to leave my comfort.

And I didn't leave with confidence. I left with questions.

When I finally said yes, I expected progress. What I got was pain. I expected elevation. What I got was excavation.

Every story of transformation includes a descent. Joseph had his pit. Jonah had his fish. Jesus had His Garden. And I had my own cave, the chamber of the heart that had to be opened so that what was dying could finally be healed.

It's strange how God answers our prayers for power by allowing weakness. I wanted authority. He gave me brokenness. I wanted a platform. He gave me a process.

Somewhere in that deep surgery of the soul, I realized He wasn't fixing something around me. He was fixing something within me.

That's the hardest truth to accept: The miracle you need isn't external. It's internal.

It took time, tears, and surrender. It took silence. It took letting go of things I thought I couldn't live without.

One of my favorite messages I've ever preached is called "Silence Is Also a Language." I didn't write that title as a slogan. I wrote it out of experience. Because there are seasons when heaven goes quiet, and you realize that God is still speaking, but now through stillness.

That silence became my classroom.

I learned that God's greatest work often happens beneath the surface, in the waiting, in the not-yet, in the hidden place where you can't prove or perform your worth.

It was in that silence that He showed me how much noise I'd built around my insecurity. How much of my faith was fueled by the need to be seen.

When He cut that away, it hurt. But it healed.

The descent led to a kind of death. The death of my control, my pride, my need to be impressive. And that death became the doorway to resurrection.

When I finally came out of that season, I didn't come out shiny. I came out scarred. I came out with a limp. But I also came out carrying something holy.

Every healed scar is a sermon.

Every limp is a testimony that God met you where you broke.

Obedience over Perfection

I tell people all the time, "God doesn't call the qualified. He qualifies the called." You may have heard that line before; I didn't come up with it myself. But I did learn it the hard way. I had to live through the disqualification before I believed the grace.

There was a point when I was ready to quit. I thought I had failed. I thought I had lost the favor of God. But in that place, I heard Him whisper, *I'm not asking for perfection. I'm asking for obedience.*

That became my new mantra: obedience over perfection.

Obedience is what keeps you moving when everything in you wants to run.

It's what turns calling into commitment, and commitment into legacy.

It's what transforms your scar into someone else's healing.

When I finally learned to obey again—to preach when I didn't feel ready, to forgive when I didn't feel safe, to keep showing up when it would've been easier to hide—I began to feel life flow through me again.

But there was still one thing keeping me from living free. It wasn't fear anymore. It was offense.

I had been hurt. Misunderstood. Betrayed. Criticized. I told myself I had forgiven, but I hadn't. I had simply built a cage and called it boundaries.

I preached about forgiveness, but inside, I was still tallying who owed me what. I didn't know it then, but offense was draining my anointing.

One day while preparing to preach a sermon, I felt the Holy Spirit interrupt me: *You can't pour clean water from a dirty pitcher.*

That's when I realized that carrying the Gospel with an offended heart is like trying to breathe with a collapsed lung. You can survive, but you can't really live.

So I forgave. Really forgave. Not with my mouth, but with my heart.

And when I did, something lifted. The air got lighter. The joy came back. The presence returned.

That's when I knew I was healed. Not because I had no scar, but because I could talk about it without pain.

Returning with the Elixir

When God heals you, He doesn't erase the evidence. He redeems it.

The Great Physician leaves His signature in every scar.

And that's how resurrection feels: like breath after suffocation, like peace after war, like laughter after years of silence.

That's when I heard God say, *Now go back. Bring what you found in the dark into the light.*

That's what the Hero's Journey calls "returning with the elixir." It's what Jesus calls the Great Commission. Either way, the meaning is the same: What you received in private, you now carry in public.

You become the medicine someone else has been praying for.

That's what the Mission 11:59 I lead is really about.[1] Not a brand, not a church expansion, but a mandate: Rescue, rebuild, release the truth again while there's still time.

We are living in the last minute before midnight. The call is no longer optional. Heaven is holding the sun in place for one more harvest.

And the Lord is whispering again, this time not to just one man, but to an entire generation, *Get up. Bring the healing home. The world is waiting.*

Every story of redemption ends in a return.
Every healed heart beats for others to live.
You go down empty, and you come up carrying life.
That's what it means to bring back the elixir.

Love Without Scorekeeping

When I finally got free from offense, I discovered that forgiveness is not the end of healing. It's the beginning of love.

Forgiveness opens the door, but love walks through it. Love is what makes freedom visible. It's what turns a theological concept into a lived reality. You can forgive someone and still keep your distance. But love? Love closes the gap. Love moves toward people, not away from them. Of course, love is always wise. Moving toward someone doesn't mean placing yourself in harm's way. In situations of abuse or danger, healthy boundaries are not a failure of love; they are an expression of it. Love can pursue the healing of a relationship while still requiring safety and accountability.

I used to think love meant fairness. If someone hurt me, I wanted balance. I wanted an apology, a correction, a clear resolution. I thought that was what it meant to have healthy boundaries. But real love doesn't keep score. It doesn't measure, compare, or demand repayment. The love of Jesus doesn't tally what it costs Him. It just gives.

That realization hit me one morning while I was journaling through another wave of frustration. I kept writing down the ways people had disappointed me: mentors who didn't show up, friends who misunderstood me, even family members who let me down. I was keeping track of everything I had given and everything I had not received in return. It was all there in black and white, proof that I had every right to feel the way I felt.

And in the middle of my pity party, I felt the Holy Spirit say, *You're doing math in a Kingdom that runs on mercy.*

That stopped me cold.

I realized I had been living like a spiritual accountant, balancing the books of my relationships. But heaven doesn't operate that way. Love doesn't count. It multiplies. It multiplies peace when it should divide. It multiplies grace when others subtract worth. It multiplies hope where bitterness wants to bankrupt the soul.

If you want to live in the freedom Jesus died for, you have to stop keeping spiritual ledgers. You have to let go of the mental spreadsheet that tracks who owes you what. Because as long as you're counting, you're still in chains.

I used to think I was protecting my boundaries, but I was actually protecting my pride. The scoreboard in my heart was proof that I still wanted control. I wanted to be the one who decided when someone had done enough to earn my love again. But that's not how God loves me. And it's not how He's asking me to love others.

Then I remembered what Paul wrote to the Corinthians—that love "keeps no record of wrongs" (1 Corinthians 13:5 NIV). That means love doesn't rehearse the offense. It doesn't replay the hurt every time that person's name comes up. It releases it. It lets it go. Not because the pain wasn't real, but because holding on to it costs more than letting it go ever could.

I mentioned earlier that my wife, Julie, kept a journal. At first, it was a record of wrongs. A place to process pain, to write down the things people had said or done that cut deep. She wasn't doing it out of spite. She was doing it honestly, because she needed to bring it into the light. She needed to know her pain was real, that she wasn't making it up or overreacting.

Later, when God began to heal her heart, she started using that journal differently. The same pages that once held offenses began to hold forgiveness. She'd go back through and write over the old entries, crossing out bitterness and replacing it with grace. One day I asked her about it, and she said, “I decided I don’t want to keep score anymore. I want to lose count.”

Those lines marked me. They still do. It was as if God was showing me, through her life, what His love really looks like. He takes our records of wrongs and turns them into records of grace. He doesn’t pretend the hurt never happened. He just refuses to let it have the last word.

Julie wasn’t ignoring the pain. She was redeeming it. She was refusing to let bitterness rewrite the story God was trying to tell through our marriage. She was choosing, again and again, to love without conditions. And somehow, that made her stronger, not weaker. Freer, not more vulnerable.

That’s the love Jesus showed on the cross. When He said, “Father, forgive them,” He wasn’t pretending the pain wasn’t real. He was declaring that love was stronger. He was choosing mercy over justice, grace over revenge, life over death. And that choice changed everything.

That kind of love is impossible without the Spirit of God. It’s not a human emotion you can manufacture. It’s divine power moving through a surrendered vessel. It’s supernatural. And that’s why you can’t fake forgiveness. You can say the words, check the religious box, go through the motions. But until your heart actually lets go, heaven knows you’re still counting.

Love without scorekeeping is the highest form of spiritual maturity. It’s how you know grace has done its work. It’s how you know your identity is no longer tied to being right, but to being redeemed. You stop needing to win. You stop needing to prove your point. You stop needing everyone to know how badly you were wronged. Because your worth doesn’t come from being the victim or the hero of the story. It comes from being loved by God.

And here’s the miracle: When you stop keeping score, you start seeing people differently.

The ones who wounded you start to look like the ones God loves. The enemies you swore to avoid start to look like the harvest you're called to reach. The person who betrayed you starts to look like someone who's also broken and in need of grace. You don't excuse what people did. You just stop letting it define them, or you.

I've seen it in ministry over and over again. Someone comes to me angry with a leader, a parent, a church. He or she is ready to quit, ready to walk away, ready to burn it all down. And I always tell that person, "You can't change what happened, but you can decide what story you tell about it."

When you choose love, you rewrite the story. When you forgive, you refuse to hand the pen to the enemy. You become part of God's story again, the one where resurrection always follows death, where beauty comes from ashes, where joy comes in the morning. And His story always ends in life, not bitterness. In freedom, not bondage. In love, not hate.

So when people ask me what revival looks like, I don't think of packed arenas or viral videos. I think of forgiveness. I think of quiet reconciliations that nobody sees, but heaven celebrates. I think of husbands and wives praying together after years of silence. I think of friendships restored, of churches healed, of hearts that finally let go of what they've been holding on to for decades.

That's revival. That's love without scorekeeping. That's what it looks like when the Kingdom of God breaks into real life.

Because love that refuses to count costs always multiplies miracles.

Sent Ones Join the Mission

When I first said yes to Jesus, I thought the goal was to be healed. Now I know healing was just the beginning.

Wholeness is not the destination. It's the qualification for being sent.

After His resurrection, Jesus appeared to the disciples and said, "As the Father has sent Me, I am sending you." Then He breathed on them and said, "Receive the Holy Spirit" (John 20:21–22 NIV). That moment has never stopped echoing through history. It still echoes in me. It's the breath I live on. The same Spirit who raised Jesus from the dead is the Spirit who now sends me out.

Every scar I carry, every tear I've shed, every lesson I've learned has become part of that sending. God wastes nothing. He takes what almost destroyed you and turns it into what equips you. The wounds you thought disqualified you become the very things that make you credible. Because people don't need someone who's never been broken. They need someone who's been put back together.

I used to believe that calling was about finding a platform. I thought it meant building something big enough for people to notice. But now I understand. Calling is not about being noticed. It's about being useful. You can be sent without a stage. You can be powerful without being popular. You can change the world without leaving your street.

The mission begins wherever your feet are standing.

When I walk into my neighborhood, I remind myself, *This is holy ground*. When I talk to my daughters, when I hug someone at church, when I speak life into a discouraged leader, I remember, *This is mission*. Every conversation is sacred. Every act of kindness is ministry. Every scar is a doorway to someone else's healing.

The world doesn't need more experts. It needs more examples. People aren't looking for perfect Christians. They're looking for whole ones. They're looking for somebody who has been through something and has come out on the other side still believing, still loving, still showing up.

That's why I keep saying, "The healed become healers." Because when Jesus restores you, He trusts you with what once broke you. The area that once disqualified you becomes the place of your authority. The thing you thought would end your ministry becomes the foundation of it.

When I was younger, I used to pray for influence. Now I pray for presence. I don't need to be everywhere. I just need to be fully where God places me. Because if I'm really there, really present, really listening, really loving, that's when heaven shows up. That's when people feel seen. That's when miracles happen in the mundane.

If I've learned anything, it's this: Mission is not about movement. It's about alignment. When your heart beats in rhythm with heaven, wherever you go, you carry the Kingdom. You don't have to chase impact. You just have to stay connected to the Source.

We're living in a generation obsessed with attention, but the Kingdom runs on *intention*. The most anointed moments of my life have not been broadcast. They've been whispered in hospital rooms, back seats, and prayer circles that no one else saw. They've happened in conversations over coffee, in text messages at midnight, in moments when someone felt alone and God used me to remind the person that he or she is not.

Sometimes people come up to me and say, "Pastor Mike, I feel called to ministry."

And I tell them, "Good. Then start today."

They usually look surprised. "But where?" they ask.

"Right where you are," I tell them. "At your job. In your home. In your circle. That's your pulpit."

You don't need a microphone to carry a message. You are the message. When the Great Physician healed your heart, He made you a living letter, written not with ink but with the Spirit of God. People read your life before they ever hear your words. And if your life says *God is real, grace works, love wins!* then you're preaching the most powerful sermon there is.

The breath of Jesus still sends people into ordinary places with extraordinary love. That's the movement I want to give my life to. Not building monuments, but multiplying miracles. Not collecting followers, but commissioning friends. Not creating a brand, but raising up a generation that knows they're sent.

We don't gather to prove that we're strong. We gather to remember that we're sent. Sent ones join the mission. We come together not to impress each other, but to encourage each other. To remind each other that we're not alone, that the mission is bigger than we are, and that God is still moving.

This is why the Mission 11:59 movement matters so deeply to me. It's not just about one church or one city. It's about the heartbeat of a generation that knows time is short, but grace is not. We're still in that last minute before midnight, and God is still holding the sun in place for one more harvest. He's saying again, *Go. Bring the healing home.*

Some will go across oceans. Some will go across the street. All are called. The mission is simple: Carry peace into chaos. Speak mercy into offense. Live as proof that grace still works. Show up when others walk away. Love when it costs you. Forgive when it's hard. Stay when it would be easier to leave.

That's what it means to join the mission.

And if your heart has been healed, then you're already qualified. You don't need another degree, another title, another platform. You just need to be willing. To say yes. To go where He sends you. To love whom He puts in front of you. To speak when He tells you to speak. To stay silent when He tells you to listen.

You're sent. Not someday. Today. Right now. Wherever you are, that's your mission field. Whomever you're with, they're your congregation. Whatever you're doing, do it as unto the Lord.

Because the mission isn't out there somewhere. It's right here. And it starts with you.

Bringing Home the Healing

When I look back over this journey, I can see how every chamber of my heart had to be opened. The brokenness, the pressure, the surrender, the resurrection. It was all preparation.

God never heals a heart just so it can beat quietly in the corner. He heals a heart so it can carry His rhythm into a world that has forgotten its song.

I used to think ministry began when I picked up a microphone. Now I know it began when I picked up my cross. Every time I forgive, I preach a sermon. Every time I love without fear, I lead a revival. Every time I choose peace instead of pride, heaven moves a little closer to earth.

That's the unoffendable life. That's the mission.

If you've walked this far with me through these pages, I believe you've felt God stirring something inside you. Maybe it started as conviction. Maybe it grew into hope. Maybe you've found words for wounds you didn't know how to name. Maybe you've cried through chapters, or had to put the book down and come back later because it was too much. That's okay. That's how healing works. It doesn't happen all at once.

But now it's time to respond.

Healing always leads to movement. Revelation always leads to release. You can't stay where you are once you've seen what is possible. You can't keep this to yourself once you've experienced it. That's not how the Kingdom works. The nature of light is to shine. The nature of life is to multiply. And the nature of a healed heart is to overflow.

So here's what I want you to ask yourself before we close: *Where will I take what I've found?*

Who around you is waiting for the love you now carry? Who needs the forgiveness that set you free? Who needs to see your scar so they can believe their wound will heal too? Because I promise you, someone needs what God just gave you. Someone in your life is stuck right where you used to be. And that person is praying for someone like you to show up. That person is praying for proof that it's possible.

The chambers of your heart are not meant to be museums of what God has done. They're meant to be rivers of what He is still doing. Don't lock up your testimony as though it's too precious to share. Don't hide your healing as though it's something to protect. Give it away. Pour it out. Let it flow. Because the more you give, the more you'll have. That's the economy of grace.

So take this healing and bring it home. Bring it to your family. Bring it to your city. Bring it to the place that still feels impossible. Be the one who carries peace into chaos. Be the one who refuses to close his or her heart. Be the one who believes love can still win.

You don't have to be perfect to be powerful. You don't have to be ready to be used. You just have to be willing. That's all God has ever asked for. Availability, not ability. A yes, not a résumé. A broken heart that has been made whole, not a flawless record.

The world is not waiting for another celebrity. It's waiting for healed people. It's waiting for someone who has been through hell and has come back with hope. It's waiting for someone who chose forgiveness when bitterness made more sense. It's waiting for someone who looks like proof that God still does miracles.

Don't Wait. . . .

If you have been healed, you're already called. The healing is the calling. The scar is the sermon. The limp is the testimony. Don't wait for permission. Don't wait for a title. Don't wait until you feel qualified. Don't wait until the conditions are perfect or the timing makes sense.

Go now. Love now. Forgive now. Speak now.

I've watched too many people wait their whole lives for the right moment, the right platform, the right opportunity. And I've learned that obedience delayed is often obedience denied. God is inviting you into something right now. Not someday. Today. This week. This moment.

The mission is waiting. And so is the world.

I don't know what that looks like for you specifically. Maybe it's a conversation you've been avoiding. Maybe it's a relationship you need to repair. Maybe it's a dream you've buried because you didn't think you were worthy. Maybe it's simply showing up differently in the life you already have.

But I know this: If you've made it this far, God has something for you to do. And He has already equipped you to do it. Every wound He healed has become a weapon in your hands. Every tear you cried has watered ground that's about to bear fruit. Every night you thought you wouldn't survive has trained you for the battles someone else is facing right now.

You are not the same person who started this book. You have been through surgery. You have walked through chambers of your own heart that you didn't even know existed. You have named things, released things, received things. And now you're standing on the other side, whole and sent.

So what will you do with this wholeness?

Will you hide it? Protect it? Keep it safe in case you need it later?

Or will you spend it? Risk it? Give it away to the first person who needs it?

Because here's what I've learned: The only way to keep what God gives you is to give it away. The moment you try to hoard grace, it stops flowing. But the moment you release it, it multiplies.

That's the heartbeat of the Kingdom. Death and resurrection. Losing and finding. Giving and receiving. Over and over and over again.

This is not the end of your story. This is the beginning of the next chapter. The one where you become the answer to someone else's prayer. The one where your mess becomes your message. The one where your test becomes your testimony.

The mission is waiting. And so is the world.

Ready to Bring Life and Healing

Take a few minutes as we close to look back over the ground we have covered. Then look forward to what joining the mission looks like for you in the days ahead. And finally, dream with God about the legacy you will leave. Thank Him, too, for where He has taken you already and for all the adventures He has planned for your future. With your chambers clear and clean, and with your heart whole and unoffendable, you are ready to bring His life and healing wherever you go.

Looking back

1. Where are you still tempted to take offense?
2. Whom do you need to forgive so you can walk free?
3. What scar in your life could become someone else's hope?
4. Which chamber of your heart felt the hardest to open, and why?
5. What pattern of offense or scorekeeping do you see in your life that you are ready to break?

Looking forward

1. What does joining the mission look like in your home, your work, your church, your city?

2. How will you carry peace into your relationships this week?
3. If you lived completely unoffendable for the next thirty days, what would change?
4. Who is one person God is asking you to reach out to with the healing you have received?
5. What would it look like for you to be "sent" right where you are, starting tomorrow?

Dreaming with God

1. If you knew you couldn't fail, what would you do with this healed heart?
2. What would your life look like five years from now if you lived from a whole heart every single day?
3. Who in your circle needs to read this book, and how will you get it to them?
4. What legacy do you want to leave as someone who chose love over offense?
5. If your heart could speak to the next generation, what would it say?

Closing Prayer

Father, thank You for healing the chambers of my heart. Thank You for the scars that remind me of Your mercy. Thank You for every incision that let in the light and made room for Your Spirit. Thank You for not leaving me where You found me.

Teach me to live unoffendable. Teach me to forgive quickly and love freely. Teach me to walk as one who has been sent. Help me remember that my healing was never just for me.

Fill me again with Your breath, the same breath that raised Jesus from the dead. Let that breath move through my words, my work, my relationships, and my worship. Let it bring life wherever I go.

Use my life to bring healing to others. Let my story become proof that grace still works. Let my scars become doorways for someone else's freedom. Let my limp become evidence that You meet us in our brokenness.

Send me now, Lord. Not when I'm ready, but while I'm willing. Not when I'm perfect, but while I'm available. Use this healed heart for Your glory.

I am ready.

Amen.

epilogue

the healed heart, the unexpected story

Some books are written merely to inform. Others are written to transform. If you have arrived at this final page, my prayer is that something unexpected and miraculous has happened inside you. Perhaps you forgave what once felt unforgivable. Perhaps wounds you thought were permanent began to heal. Perhaps you confronted what had tormented you for years, and in doing so, you became a clearer reflection of Christ Jesus.

You are not the same person who opened this book. Somewhere along the journey, the Holy Spirit extended a quiet invitation, and you had the courage to say yes. That yes carried you through every chapter, and it may be one of the most significant choices you have ever made.

Maybe you began this book scarred, skeptical, and worn down from carrying the heavy ledger of offenses you had been keeping in the secret places of your heart. Yet you continued to turn the pages. That's what makes you different. Despite everything you have endured, you refused to stay stuck. Offense once promised you a sense of power, but now you have discovered a greater power—the power of the cross and the power to tell a better story.

This book concludes here, but your story continues. You will experience hurt again. The difference now is that offense is no longer an automatic reaction. It has become a choice. Your heart is not perfect, yet it is healed and still healing under the faithful hands of the One who restores you.

The Scriptures say "Satan entered into" Judas (John 13:27). The Greek verb used here, *eiserchomai*, carries the sense of entering with force—it describes an intrusion rather than a gentle arrival.[1] Judas cracked the door of his heart through bitterness and resentment, and the enemy didn't simply stroll through that opening. He pushed his way in. It was the violent entry of darkness into a heart that had allowed offense to linger, even under a perfect leader. Judas didn't fall in a single moment. He surrendered piece by piece, until the door that should have been shut in vigilance was left unlocked. What happened next wasn't subtle. It was the spiritual equivalent of a door being kicked off its hinges.

Your heart is different.

Your heart chooses to close what Judas opened. Your heart chooses mercy instead of memory, grace instead of grievance, and healing instead of hurt. You have refused to let offense determine your destiny. Your heart now beats with the power of the Holy Spirit—the same power that raised Christ from the dead, and the same power that enables you to forgive again and again.

This strength is not your own. It is His strength at work in you. Your life is living proof that when God rewrites a story, the last chapter can be better than the first. You have turned the page. You have stepped into freedom. You have become a testimony that offense does not have to rule over you.

You carry something rare now.

Something sacred.

Something strong enough to change every relationship and every room you walk into.

You carry *the unoffendable heart*.

notes

Chapter 2 Expectations: The Ledger of Disappointment

1. Viktor Frankl, *Man's Search for Meaning* (Beacon Press, 2006), 47.

Chapter 3 Justice: Why Your Heart Keeps Score

1. For the Hebrew and Greek definitions throughout, I am drawing primarily from standard lexical sources widely used in biblical studies. The definitions are not original to me, but are concise summaries of established lexical ranges. In this case, my definition of *mishpat* (מִשְׁפָּט) is drawn from *Strong's Exhaustive Concordance of the Bible* H4941, which defines the term as judgment, justice, ordinance, or sentence. This aligns with the *Brown-Driver-Briggs Hebrew Lexicon*, which includes meanings such as judgment, decision, or legal verdict. My phrasing "ruling or verdict" is a condensed rendering of that range.

2. My definition of *tsedeq* (צֶדֶק / צְדָקָה) is drawn from *Strong's Concordance* H6664 and is supported by *Brown-Driver-Briggs*. The term refers to righteousness, rightness, or conformity to a standard. The underlying Hebrew imagery includes the idea of something being straight or upright, which is why I rendered it as "straight or right."

3. My definition of *ekdikēsis* (ἐκδίκησις) is drawn from *Strong's Concordance* G1557 and also the *Greek-English Lexicon of the New Testament and Other Early Christian Literature* (known as the BDAG) and *Thayer's Greek-English Lexicon of the New Testament*. This word carries meanings such as vengeance, retribution, or vindication. My phrasing "justice carried out" reflects the sense of justice being executed, not just defined.

4. Martin Luther King Jr., *Strength to Love* (Harper & Row, 1963), 47.

Chapter 4 Confidence: The Fear of People's Opinions

1. My definition of *pachad* (פַּחַד) is drawn from *Strong's Concordance* H6342.
2. My definition of *moqesh* (ומֹקֵשׁ) is drawn from *Strong's Concordance* H4170.
3. My definition of *areskō* (ἀρέσκω) is drawn from *Strong's Concordance* G700.
4. My definition of *doxa* (δόξα) is drawn from *Strong's Concordance* G1391.

5. My definition of *qōl* (לקו) is drawn from *Strong's Concordance* H6963.

6. My definition of *dābār* (רָבָד) is drawn from *Strong's Concordance* H1697.

7. For more on the original Greek phrase from Matthew 22:16 and its meaning, see *Strong's Concordance* G4383, referring to the Greek word *prosōpon* (πρόσωπον), which means face or countenance. The Greek vocabulary resources found at https://www.billmounce.com were also helpful, along with the Bible Hub lexicon entry found at https://biblehub.com/lexicon/matthew/22-16.htm.

Chapter 5 Memory: The Past That Won't Let Go

1. My definition of *chazaq* (קָזַח) is drawn from *Strong's Concordance* H2388. See also Bible Hub's lexicon entry found at https://biblehub.com/lexicon/joshua/1-9.htm. As the text notes, this word carries the sense of fastening or clinging to something external—in context, to the faithfulness of God—rather than summoning courage from within oneself.

2. Dr. Maté has stated this in numerous interviews and lectures, and the quote is widely attributed to him in this form, but see also his book *In the Realm of Hungry Ghosts: Close Encounters with Addictions* (North Atlantic Books, 2010).

3. Neil T. Anderson and Mike & Julia Quarles, *Freedom from Addiction* (Bethany House, 1996), 314. Fore more on strongholds, see also Neil T. Anderson, *The Bondage Breaker* (Harvest House, 2019).

Chapter 6 Going Deep into the Heart

1. *Star Wars: Episode V—The Empire Strikes Back*, directed by Irvin Kershner (Twentieth Century-Fox/Lucasfilm Ltd., 1980).

Chapter 8 Surrender Is Not a Sidenote

1. My definition of *akoloutheō* (ἀκολουθέω) is drawn from *Strong's Concordance* G190.

2. My definition of *kenoō* (κενόω) is drawn from *Strong's Concordance* G2758.

3. My definition of *hupakoē* (ὑπακοή) is drawn from *Strong's Concordance* G5218.

Chapter 10 Joining the Mission

1. For more on the Mission 11:59 movement, see https://mikesignorelli.com/mike-writes/why-i-believe-theres-still-time-the-mission-1159-movement.

Epilogue: The Healed Heart, the Unexpected Story

1. My definition of *eiserchomai* (εἰσέρχομαι) is drawn from *Strong's Concordance* G1525.

Mike Signorelli

is a pastor, filmmaker, content creator, author, philanthropist, and speaker. His humble beginnings growing up in impoverished Chicagoland motivated him to pursue higher education and eventually to answer the call to preach and lead.

Mike is the pastor and founder of V1 Church, a vibrant and growing community of believers around the world, with physical church locations in Long Island, Brooklyn, Manhattan, New Jersey, Miami, and northwest Indiana. Mike also has a global church community with hundreds of online watch parties meeting weekly. V1 Church was listed at No. 26 in *Outreach* magazine's "Outreach 100 Fastest-Growing Churches" in America in 2023, while INJOY Stewardship Solutions called it the "fastest-growing church in America" for five years running.

Mike started a teaching broadcast during the COVID-19 pandemic that grew to over five million viewers per month across social platforms. As a result, V1 College was established to provide leadership and theological training, and currently has more than two hundred students enrolled from over twenty nations. He also developed The Breakers App, which offers training worldwide in the basics of evangelism, healing, prophecy, and deliverance ministry.

After escaping the poverty of his early years, Mike was motivated to help young families thrive. Seeing many people struggle for basic necessities in New York City Metro, he and his wife, Julie, responded by creating a nonprofit called V1 Community

Impact. This foundation provides a Christmas miracle to hundreds of people in shelters between Brooklyn and Long Island. In addition, hundreds of families receive food monthly through its philanthropic work.

In 2023, Mike wrote and directed the movie *The Domino Revival*, based on his own life story. The film played in over one thousand theaters nationwide, and moviegoers experienced healing, deliverance, and salvation; some even canceled suicides. Mike has also published several books well received by audiences around the world. Aside from his work as a content creator, filmmaker, pastor, author, and philanthropist, Mike is also a sought-after speaker who travels the world speaking at church gatherings, conferences, tent revivals, and festivals.

For Mike and Julie, family remains at the core of their work. They have two daughters, Everly Faith and Bella Joy. They currently reside in New York City.

Connect with Mike

MikeSignorelli.com

PsMikeSignorelli

@MikeSignorelli_

@MikeSignorelli_

Personal Notes: Healing My Heart

Personal Notes: Healing My Heart

Personal Notes: Healing My Heart

www.ingramcontent.com/pod-product-compliance
Lightning Source LLC
LaVergne TN
LVHW081023041126
851710LV00020B/64

* 9 7 8 0 8 0 0 7 7 2 6 1 1 *